HiLLBiLLY QUEER

A MEMOIR

J.R. JAMISON

the facing project

THE FACING PROJECT PRESS
An imprint of The Facing Project
Muncie, Indiana 47305
facingproject.com

First published in the United States of America by The Facing Project
Press, an imprint of The Facing Project and division of The Facing Project
Gives Inc., 2021.

First paperback edition May 2021

Cover design by Emma Fulkerson & Shantanu Suman
Cover photography by Brock Williamson
Author photography by Matt Howell

Library of Congress Control Number: 2020946996

ISBN: 978-1-7345581-6-6 (paperback)
ISBN: 978-1-7345581-7-3 (eBook)

Printed in the United States of America

10 9 8 7 6 5 4 3 2 1

For all the kids out there in the middle of nowhere who feel like they don't belong.

We do not grow absolutely, chronologically. We grow sometimes in one dimension, and not in another; unevenly. We grow partially. We are relative. We are mature in one realm, childish in another.

The past, present, and future mingle and pull us backward, forward, or fix us in the present. We are made up of layers, cells, constellations.

—Anaïs Nin

AUTHOR'S NOTE

To be a writer of memoir is to put oneself, and the experiences one writes about, on the page the best way one knows how—from memory. Because of that, there is nuance in the way views are expressed and captured through time. What one person may remember from an exact moment can vary greatly from how someone else recalls what occurred. This book is based on my memories and mine alone from my experiences, including stories told to me, from childhood to the present.

The events and conversations in this book have been set down to the best of my ability; although some names and details have been changed to protect the privacy of individuals, and some of the scenes and dialogue have been condensed, combined, or altered to fit the length of a book and the narrative arc of this story. In some instances, minor composite characters and situations have been created to move the narrative forward; but none of these occurrences take away from the underlying thesis or truth of this particular story.

I have done my best to remain fair in the retelling of my life from my experiences. I have lived forty-one years on this planet, my dad seventy-seven, and our full time together, and the history of our lives and the people who have intersected with us, cannot be captured in 250 to 300 pages. There are more stories to share, and different ways to share them, that are not included in this book. As a writer, my greatest wish is to cause harm to no one, but to tell stories in a way that connect people, create conversation, and challenge perceptions.

INTRODUCTION

If good ole boy, straight-shooting, deer hunter, or a man's man are words that describe my dad, then, well, I'm everything opposite of that. I'm more of a gay-as-the-day-is-long don't shoot anything kind of man's man. I spend my days in the world of trigger warnings and safe spaces, while my blue-collar dad spends his yelling "snowflakes!" at the TV and questioning how America has become so sensitive. There's always been this difference between us, and as I've gotten older I've come to realize that what we represent is the rising divide in our nation. Two people on either end of the political spectrum: a conservative, a liberal; a hillbilly, a queer; but also, a dad and a son.

Growing up, my hometown of Cowan, Indiana, wasn't a place where those like me felt at home. It wasn't a place where one could sip a single-origin-red-eye coffee while getting lost among the melting clocks of a Dalí and contemplate lives laid bare to the passage of time. Cowan's claim to

fame was the *Street Light Festival,* the biggest cultural expo-
sition this side of the Norfolk Southern Railway.

During the nights of the festival train cars filled with
coal and cattle would tear across the tracks, sounding a
whistle that disappeared into the darkness as the townsfolk
sat at booths selling crochet blankets and homemade peanut
brittle to raise enough money to keep the street lights on—all
four of them. I spent those nights staring beyond the tracks
and knew that somewhere down the twisted line, miles
away, were exotic places like New York City and Los Ange-
les. For most kids, I imagine there's a longing for somewhere
different; but for gay kids who grow up in flyover country
there's more than a longing—we know those tracks and roads
can lead us to freedom.

I never imagined I'd actually make it down those tracks
and leave. I never thought I'd grow up to be an academic
who would be sent to far off places like China to research,
and that my storytelling practices would lead to having my
own program on NPR, and that one day I'd get to marry
another man who loves me as much as I love him. But I did.
Yet twenty years after I'd left Cowan, a phone call brought
me back to the center of conservative country.

Mom asked that I come home for Dad's seventy-second
birthday dinner. Life hadn't been kind to him the past few
years. He'd slowed down; crept through the house slightly
hunched over; complained about pain in his left knee while
he gripped it with arthritic hands. He reminisced about days
gone by more and more. It all drove Mom crazy. She wanted
someone else to sit with him for a bit. I wasn't sure how
much longer he'd be around, so I told her I'd come.

The interesting thing about the passage of time is that place and space become an optical illusion of sorts. Some things, on the surface, appear the same even though deep down, if looked at closely, the changes are right in front of us. As I drove around Cowan, the same pot hole near the high school—that I had to swerve to miss each day on my drive there—still waited for an unsuspecting tire. The Jiffy Mart's sign still hung along Main Street; though long ago the store closed, its decaying building with peeling paint had fallen away with the memories of the town.

At my parents' home I sat across from Dad at the same kitchen table where he found the love letter from my boyfriend twenty years before. The letter that outed me and made the gap between us even wider. Aside from clinks on the side of serving dishes, there was silence as we passed around the mashed potatoes.

Dad furrowed his brow and sucked on his teeth. "What do you think of that Trump?"

"I think you know what I think. He's kind of a charlatan," I said with a chuckle.

Dad scooped a heaping forkful of green beans into his mouth and swallowed without chewing. "Well, he'll do a good job for people in these parts. Don't you think?"

I picked at my mashed potatoes and let my mind get lost among the blue flowers along the edges of the CorningWare so I didn't have to answer. Over the last several years, Dad and I had made a concerted effort to reconnect and not fight about our differences; but rather find common ground as our jumping off point for conversation and debate. But it was hard. Despite being connected by blood, most of our philosophies on life did not, well, connect. Many of our phone calls had long gaps of silence as I struggled to find words to say. It would have been easy to hang up, but Dad wouldn't let me slip away and always changed the topic to keep me.

"I ever tell you about the time I thought I was Superman?"

I looked up from my plate and tried to understand. I saw an old man with sagging jowls and silver hair before me. Not the dad from my childhood. I studied his craggy face and he smiled proudly despite the tobacco stains that lined the grooves of his teeth. "I jumped from a tree. Thought I could fly, so I went ahead and jumped."

I tried to picture Dad as this daring child, but I couldn't. I *could* remember the days when he was a version of the man I knew best: middle-aged, salt-and-pepper, sporting a dad-bod with a little more tone and a wad of tobacco bulging from his lower lip. But even my mind in its most creative moments couldn't picture him as a child. He'd always been a grown-up to me. And now he'd grown older than ever and my memories of him with that dad-bod were only that . . . images of a time gone by. I wondered if he feared death, and I wanted to ask, but I couldn't muster the courage. I couldn't imagine him *not* here, even though I'd only allowed him to be tangentially "here" for many years.

"Did you get hurt?" I asked instead.

"I racked myself on a picket fence. Let's just say it wasn't as *super* as I had imagined."

I giggled thinking about Dad straddling the fence, dressed as Superman, clutching his balls in pain and wishing he hadn't taken the leap. I asked for another story, and silently wished I'd get a few more years with this man of steel.

He leaned in and, with a glint of excitement in his eyes, asked if I'd like to take a trip. One back in time to the place where he grew up in rural, central Missouri for his fifty-five year class reunion. A place that I knew was deep in Trump-country, and if I said yes our time together would be more in his territory than mine.

Our eyes fixed on each other and I nodded with a nervous and uncertain smile, still picking at my mashed potatoes hoping to find the answer buried within. We hadn't spent any quality time together in nearly two decades; yet, our phone calls and short visits over the years allowed us to tip-toe into each other's worlds enough to stick around for the next phone call and the next visit.

When I was born, Dad was five years younger than I am now. When you become older than the age your parents were when you were born, mortality begins to set in. The past few years I'd caught myself staring into any reflective surface, examining creases on my forehead, cringing at the crow's feet darting from my eyes. There's not enough eye serum or coconut oil in the world to stop the inevitable. And each time my husband cuts my hair, he reminds me the gray has rippled its way around my head in a half circle. A loss of pigmentation, a gain of distinguish, a harrowing acceptance that I'm now middle-aged. And when I looked at Dad, silver hair, hunched over, telling stories and longing for his glory days, it pained me. I will be him someday; his age—yearning for the way things once were.

But can we ever really find our way back to each other? Can we change things from the past?

Going back to my hometown of Cowan was both crushing and empowering. Before sitting down for Dad's birthday dinner I decided to traverse the roads I'd once traveled each day. Like muscle memory, I knew each turn and curve like the back of my hand; but those familiar roads also held painful memories and led to the unlocked doors of my high school. I let myself in and walked the halls. Only four hallways that created a square with the gymnasium in the middle. I'd stood on stages in auditoriums larger than its gym and entertained crowds twice the size of my entire high school.

Why was I ever afraid of this place?

And then echoes from many years before screeched past me and circled back around; they spun me into fear and confusion. "Faggot!" "Homo!" A chill rushed through my veins. The same kids who walked those halls with me and called me those names likely grew up to be the people who chanted at the Trump rallies I'd seen on TV. They never really went away. They were always there in the back of my mind, haunting me, reminding me that I'm this thing that's different. Going home can zap all the confidence you've built up over time and take you back to being that kid again who stared down the tracks for something bigger. You look around and feel the memories permeating all of your senses and realize that these spaces—and some of the people there—still hold you down.

But maybe it was me? What if I were the one who couldn't let go of the past? What if I were part of the problem?

Even before Trump took the podium and started chanting "Build the wall" and "Lock her up," I'd felt a growing divide in our country. Us vs. them. I was *us* and people like Dad were *them*. We'd set up our own camps and allowed our differences to separate us. But the years of age that had fallen on both of our faces had taught me that we can't make up for lost time but tomorrow is always a new day and we could try to find our way back to each other. But could our differences bring us closer together or would they push us further apart?

I mean, after all, we were two people who should not like each other. People like me looked at people like Dad and thought, "Hillbilly." And people like Dad looked at people like me and thought, "Queer." But maybe this once we could be brave enough to go beyond conversations and step wildly into each other's worlds. What would we find on the other side?

Maybe we'd find that the divide in our country—between people like us—was inevitable and it'd be best to keep our distance. Or maybe we'd find that it takes courage to step outside of our comfort zones—to pop our liberal and conservative bubbles—and we'd find we're more alike than we are different.

I poked some more at my mashed potatoes while I contemplated those thoughts. Dad smiled again, flashing his tobacco-stained teeth. I looked down at my Bella Canvas fair trade t-shirt and looked back up at Dad in his Hanes Camo with tiny holes that lined the neck.

"I'll go," I said.

He nodded with suspicion.

Unlike Dad standing in that tree as a child, contemplating what to do and where his leap might take him, I'd been afraid to fall completely with abandon. But this time, with Dad, we're going to jump together—to see where it might take us and to see what it's really like on the other side. A distance in age, experience, politics, and twenty years' worth of miles.

1

Surrounded by a sea of concrete in a parking lot of a road-side motel, I placed my distressed leather, hand-stitched safari travel bag on the ground at my feet. A vagabond who wore *Jesus Saves* on his camo hat, and who had dirt in the cracks of his forehead, shuffled across the lot to ask for a light. I shook my head and waved him off, my *Cartier Love* bracelet glistened in the sunlight. This shit-hole would be home for the next four days.

The sun radiated off of the parking lot and reminded me it was the hottest day of the year. I never knew how hot 103 degrees was until the only thing that separated me from the scorching misery below was a thin layer of rubber otherwise known as flip-flops.

I stretched my arms above my head, turned side to side, and took in the scenery around me. A couple of breakfast joints that looked like they used to be a Shoney's or a Denny's, a weathered truck stop, and the motel that stood two stories tall. The weed-filled lot around me had more parking spaces than cars and trucks to fill those spaces, and the thistle and nettle that reached for sunlight through the cracks made me pretty certain some of the spots hadn't seen a vehicle in years.

I asked Dad what year this place was built.

He squinted his eyes in contemplation. "I'd say they built it in about '80, if I'm remembering right. It's the only halfway decent place to stay around here. Ain't no places over in Steelville."

I stared at the dented row of paint-chipped rusty doors along the parking lot's edge and wondered how many people had been murdered here. Clearly Dad's definition of "decent" was not the same as mine. Then I had an even scarier thought: BED BUGS. I've had a fear of bed bugs for about four years. My office is in the basement of a residence hall on a college campus that had a bed bug outbreak. Ever since then, I can't stay anywhere without doing a thorough inspection of the room. I even travel with bed bug spray. Some say I'm fairly neurotic, but it can take years to rid your home of those little buggers if one hops a ride with you.

Inside, the motel wasn't as bad as the sorry state of its parking lot. The lobby hadn't been updated since the 90s, but at least it had been kept up. Silk floral swags and *Home Interior* paintings of pastel angels, in blues and mauves, hung on the wall. A shabby-chic coffee table surrounded by an over-stuffed floral couch and love seat pointed the way to a tube TV in a pressed-pine wood entertainment center. I'll admit, I was a little judge-y.

I'd been spoiled the past several years and had stayed mainly at Westin's and JW Marriott's for my work. When I could find an off-the-beaten-path boutique hotel, I'd call that my home for a few days. On my own dime, I usually booked the Hampton or stayed at an upscale Airbnb with those little *no smoking* signs in gold-lamé frames. This kind of motel was definitely a first for me, at least in several years. Dad would stay in the woods if he could. The MRSA he got from a deer-hunting camp shower in southern Indiana wasn't enough to keep him from going back.

"Can I help you?" A woman with a gruff voice called out from behind the counter. Her feathered hair on top met a permed bottom below her ears. Her nametag read: RHONDA.

"Yes, Ma'am!" Dad laughed as he approached the counter. "My boy and me are heading to my fifty-five year class reunion, and—"

"I'm guessing you have a reservation?"

"Yeah. You know, I haven't been down this way in some time, and the last time was for my fiftieth—"

"Last name?"

"Should be under Jamison. This is the motel where most the folks stay. Has anybody else coming to the reunion checked in yet?"

"We've had a couple."

"How about some of those Connor boys? I played basket—"

"Sir, I'm not from around these parts. I came here in '86 with my husband, Frank. He got a job driving a truck. So, I don't know nobody from high school days."

"Well, we had one of the best basketball teams in the state of Missouri—"

Rhonda cut him off again and gave us her best bored

3

look. "I've got you in Room 10. Go out this door here to the parking lot, turn right, and you're the third door down."

Dad turned to me and opened his eyes wide and smiled. Embarrassed but not willing to accept defeat. It was clear Rhonda didn't want to hear his stories and I felt bad for him. An old man with stories no one wanted to hear.

Dad had always been known in our family for his stories, animated and captivating, but to be completely honest I understood Rhonda. She was doing her job, counting down the hours until her next smoke break; no time for small talk. When I was a kid, I was too busy watching *Fraggle Rock* and *Saved by the Bell* to listen to Dad's stories. Now, as an adult, I'd grown too impatient because it seemed Dad had a way of holding people hostage with his words. *Loneliness?* Maybe. I don't know. After I'd heard the same stories over and over, it was nearly impossible for me not to fall back into the old habit of drowning them out.

But, of course, it was easy to remember my favorite story of his. The one he loved to retell time and again—the one he forced on me and my siblings so often that we knew it line by line. The one where he tried his hand at attending a small Bible college, but he was asked to leave after a semester because of the dynamite incident. As in, he and one of his buddies got their hands on a stick of dynamite and thought it would be the greatest of all pranks if—deep into finals week in the wee hours of the night—they lit the said stick of dynamite and threw it into the grassy quad. The result: one huge hole in the ground and a fellow student sent to the hospital with minor injuries.

Now, in today's day and age, that type of incident would not only be grounds for expulsion but a criminal offense. In 1961 Missouri, it was only considered bad form and he was asked to leave the academy with no chance he'd ever be invited back. Little did he know at the time, that hole in the ground would leave a 50-year-old hole in his life.

Dad had other stories that were so played out and retread that, whenever he launched into one of them, I maintained eye contact but my ears developed the hyperability to hear every other conversation happening in the room. I would see Dad's mouth move but wouldn't make out any words. Other than eye contact, I would give an obligatory, "Oh, really," and "Hmm . . . yeah, that's interesting."

Those were the stories that focused on Dad's basketball and track records, or the stories of his great-grandfather, Wild Devil Jim Jamison, a Missouri outlaw who road with Quantrill's Raiders (a group of bandits that included Jesse James). In the last year, he'd added a new story. A story about a man who he thought could save America—Donald Trump. And it was those stories about our corrupt wannabe commander in chief that made me completely shut down.

As a gay man who had spent most of my adult life traveling the world and meeting people of different backgrounds, Dad's stories of small town Missouri life weren't that interesting to me. And his love for the loud-mouthed blowhard who ran for President made it even harder to listen.

I'd spent much of my life unconnected from his stories, but on the car ride to Missouri I decided to see, and feel, the emotion behind them; to try to find a connection between our lives. As I stared out onto I-70, the stretch of road that carried us to Missouri and the same road that took Dad to Indiana to start his new life so many years before, I actually listened for the first time to Dad's track record story. With a captive audience, Dad darted his eyes from me to the road to me to the road. The smile never dropped from his face.

He told me he held the record at Steelville High School for the 120-yard high hurdles. He ran them in 14.9 seconds and the only person who could beat him in the state of Missouri was this boy from over in Jefferson City. "But they took that from me. When they did away with yards and converted to meters, they just packed up my record and probably put it in storage next to the brooms and cleaning supplies."

He gripped the steering wheel tighter.

"Why would they do something like that?" I asked.

"They told me they only display records for current sporting events."

"Did you ask if you could have the record, for your own keeping?"

He paused and laughed. "Yeah. They told me it was 'lost.'"

I thought back to my own high school involvement, which didn't live in the world of sports but in Drama Club. I'd be pissed if that happened to me, but there weren't trophies for best acting. And trophies hadn't meant as much to me, anyhow.

High school was not glory days for me. I wasn't Mr. Popular like Dad, even when I tried my hand at student clubs. I was a gangly gay kid in rural Indiana who couldn't fit in. Even though I had never spoken the words to anyone but myself, all the other kids knew it. Kids have that strange psychic ability, and, when there were fewer than 300 students in my school, their intuitions had become truths that traveled fast and the repercussions weren't pretty.

One time in the locker room after gym class, another kid threw an empty spray deodorant canister at my head, narrowly missing only because I ducked. He then positioned his hands in a triangle around his dick. "I bet you can suck it real good, faggot. Why don't you come over here and give it a try."

The laughter and whoops were broken by our gym teacher, Mr. Cochran, who entered stage right. I could hear Dad's tough voice in my head telling me to take the other kid out, "Punch that son-of-a-bitch right in the mouth!"

I wasn't brave enough to do it. Unlike Dad, I wasn't a fighter, so I gathered my belongings and exited stage left.

But these memories don't go away. They linger in your mind and take swings at you when things start to get better. Not so gentle reminders of who you really are and from where you came.

Dad interrupted my own trip down memory lane. "Even though they packed it away, that record won me a scholarship to Southeast Missouri State."

I was stunned. Either that was a story I failed to listen to in the past, or Dad had dropped another bomb and unleashed a secret he'd kept for over fifty years. I turned toward him, his eyes darted from the road ahead back to my own. He told me he heard his name blared over the PA system: *Dave Jamison, you're needed in the Principal's*

Office. He saw his Coach with a clipboard and paper in hand, smile from ear to ear, who stood with some man in a three-piece suit. "Just sign on the dotted line," they told him.

Leaving Steelville behind was on his mind, but he thought maybe he could hold on to the past a little longer and sort some things out and help his Dad at the grocery. He kept wondering why he had to sign the offer that day. "Couldn't it wait?"

With no direction other than a pen that guided him toward the dotted line, he handed the clipboard back over and told them *no.* The grins dropped from the men's faces. The recruiter folded his arms. And just like that, he gave up his chance to get a full ride to Southeast Missouri State.

I studied his face, expressionless, but his eyes held a sense of reflection and sadness.

"Do you regret it?"

Dad blew air through his nose and waved off this memory with his hand. "If I had gone there who knows where I'd be today. I might not even have you." He leaned toward my side of the car, wrapped his arm around my shoulders, and gave me a hard pat. He smiled, but it fell away as soon as it appeared.

I found it all hard to believe. How could he not regret the chance he had to be a star on the college track? Did he never wonder what life would've been like with trophies and handshakes and photo opportunities? He had lived a part of his adult life on the road, but it was a life spent with greased hands that inspected valves on the pipeline; not a life that smiled for the cameras.

"So how'd you end up at Bible college?"

"Roger." He laughed and shook his head at the mention

of his older brother. "Roger was headed there and he convinced me to go. 'Oh, come on, Dave, it'll be fun,' he told me. 'We'll room together and it will be a big party.' Well, yeah, that's what he said but he quickly got a girlfriend, knocked her up, and he was gone in no time."

Roger is older by only a year. Dad was born in a doctor's home in St. James, Missouri, in 1944. Grandma was pregnant with triplets and the babies hung on to survival as they made their way into the world. And only one of them did survive. *Dad.*

The birth and death of two of her three babies left Grandma bed-ridden for more than a year. Grandpa took care of Dad, but he ran his own gas station and grocery and he had his own priorities with the bottle. That didn't leave much time to watch after two kids. So Roger was sent to live with Grandpa's parents and by the time Grandma was better Roger didn't want to come back. Dad and Roger grew up more like cousins than brothers. And when they were in junior high, Roger and Dad's grandparents made the move to Indiana for work on the Gulf pipeline and Dad pretty much grew up from there as an only child. Going to Bible college together was a time for them to rediscover themselves as brothers. But a pregnancy sent Roger, along with his girl, back to Indiana, and the dynamite incident sent Dad following him.

"Boy, Dad and Mom were so mad at me about that, they called up Grandpa, got me a job, and within a week I was gone."

IN THE MOTEL LOBBY, Rhonda called out as we headed to our room. "And if you need a map of the area, we have some back over in that rack with the travel brochures."

I walked over to the rack and found a hand-drawn map. Certainly not to scale. Someone had literally taken the time to draw out each street and intersection in the town along with identifying landmarks. In the lower right-hand corner, in the same handwriting, it read in all seriousness: Cuba, Missouri, © 2014. Beneath the map lay several more copies for the other weary occupants and explorers of this small Missouri town.

Outside of the motel, we counted the numbers on the rusty doors until we reached *Room 10*, where the key wouldn't work.

"Son of a bitch," Dad swore as he jiggled the handle. The green light illuminated and the knob turned, but the door wouldn't budge. "Give it a kick," he instructed.

I reared back my flip-flopped right foot and exposed a dark, cavernous, and musty scene on the other side of the door. We were lured inside by the welcoming coolness of the humming window unit. Dad pulled back the curtain. "Let's get some light on this situation."

I slipped into pest control mode. I went to the beds, threw the pillows to the floor, and ripped off the comforters and sheets. My thumb pulled down the piping on the mattresses as my forefinger inspected every crack, corner, and crevice to make sure our room was bug free. I then opened the drawer to the nightstand because that's where they often like to hide. I squirted a thick layer of bed bug spray over the bedding.

"Are we good?" Dad chuckled.

"We're good."

We sat on opposite beds and faced each other. Complete silence for the first time in several hours as the late-afternoon sun shone into the room and traced shadows across the navy blue carpet.

Connected *but* strangers.

I had begun to relearn how to listen to Dad—how to make eye contact and actually listen—and our DNA undeniably shared some of the same blocks, but I couldn't help but think about his love for Trump and how when we were back in Cowan I had told him I thought Trump was a charlatan. And it felt like he hadn't listened to me; that he hadn't cared what I actually thought. I couldn't move past the idea that his love for that man could impact my life as a gay man; that it could overturn policies and laws toward the negative in ways that he'd never in his life had to consider. And I remembered he told me when I was only a boy that AIDS was punishment for the gays sent down by God.

These thoughts echoed inside of my brain and wouldn't turn off. These thoughts continued to create a wedge between us, at least in my mind.

I texted my husband Cory: HELP! WHY DID I AGREE TO DO THIS?

Dad stood and searched for the remote. "How about we turn on that Fox News and see what Trump's up to?"

Hell no. "How about we grab something to eat. I'm pretty hungry."

Strangers, that's what we were. Strangers who had no business sharing a room together, especially if one of us planned to hole up all night watching right-wing propaganda on the television.

Dad looked at me slightly confused, eyes cocked to the side. For the first time since that morning I decided I was done listening, and it only took eight hours. I think he recognized my shift. I didn't want to watch Fox News and I wasn't ready to hear stories I didn't agree with about a man who I loathed. Donald Trump promised to make America great again, and he vied to be the 45th President of the United States on a platform of hate.

I studied the shadows on the floor and contemplated my decision to come on this trip.

Cory texted back: STAY. I threw my phone beside me on the bed.

Dad remained standing. I stayed seated. The silence stretched on as we searched for something else to say. We had twenty years of road to cover in only a few days, but nothing seemed to find its way to the tip of our tongues at the right time in the right way. It hadn't been this way with Mom. As I'd gone home over the years and made phone calls to them on the weekends, Mom and I always had something to say to one another. She and I had grown closer with time. With Dad, the space between us continued to grow and grow; with less and less to say. But it hadn't always been that way. When and where did we go wrong? Had he built the divide? Or had I?

I studied the old carpet of the motel room and searched for answers, or, perhaps, a sign that the room did indeed have bed bugs. That could have been my out to hit the road. Other than that, I wasn't sure what to look for anyway. I had been without direction on figuring out Dad for a long time.

But what had he been running from all of these years?
Was it me?

And what exactly was he running to?

Was it the past?

Those were questions I could have asked of myself.

Connected *but* strangers. We had nothing more than time and that hand-drawn map to help us change that fact.

2

"I THINK this is where we turn off if I remember right," Dad said, uncertain.

That uncertainty was validated as we turned down a road that led us into an industrial park. It was a long stretch of tired pavement that fingered off into cul-de-sac dead-ends, factories and warehouses along each phalanx. I immediately knew this was not the right way, but I decided not to tell Dad until we turned down a dead end for the third time. At this rate, the burger that called my name wasn't going to find its way to my stomach any time soon.

I tried to make sense of the hand-drawn map from the motel, turning it from side to side. *Fuck, I'm not sure that north is actually north on this damned thing.*

Then I realized, out of all the buildings sketched with a steady hand and a Number 2 pencil, the industrial park had been left off. I assumed the wannabe cartographer determined it was neither a tourist attraction nor an important identifying landmark. Dad, in his most determined voice, called it like he finally saw it. "Yeah, I don't think this is right."

We pulled back onto the highway and one block up found the old road that had been there all along. He knew exactly where we were going. I wasn't much help with that hand-drawn map.

We darted down the dirt road, dust swirled around the car and created a reddish brown veil over land and sky. Dad recalled stories about coming down this road every day when he was a teenager. He pointed to a low-lying field off to the right, barely visible through the dust settled on the window, and told a story about baling hay one summer and being chased out by a copperhead.

"Boy, I jumped that wire fence down there so fast and my foot got caught in one of the top squares—"

He slammed on the breaks and brought the car to a sudden halt. Dust swirled around in one last dance and dropped before us and out of sight. I could see clearly now and realized how rural we were. Off to the right sat the low-lying field surrounded by a large-squared wire fence with weathered wooden posts every ten feet. Fifty or more round bales of hay stood at attention. Off to the left was a tree-lined bluff with an over-grown gravel drive that headed straight up the side into a tunnel of darkness.

Dad pointed toward the drive and followed it with his finger up to the sky. "Do you see that there, Joe? Do you see it?"

I searched the wooded area and expected to see a mountain lion or a deer or the camo Jesus guy from the motel, but I couldn't make out much beyond the thick foliage other than what remained of the gravel drive. Dad asked if I thought we could make it. I stared ahead and tried to make sense of what he said and what I saw. "You mean, up there?"

Dad chuckled and shook his head yes. He continued to look beyond the drive and the foliage and remembered something that was once there. He told me his old girlfriend, Barbara, lived up that way. Nights of dinners filled with venison and farm-fresh green beans must have danced in his head. The slow illumination of the oil lamp he saw in his vision faded away as he put the car into *Drive*. We rolled forward toward the base of the bluff. Before us the gravel path led into overgrowth so thick the trees on either side had met in the middle. It was a tunnel into oblivion and Dad's past. He pushed hard on the gas and catapulted us forward. Our heads jerked from side to side as weeds whipped against the doors in a failed attempt to hold us back.

"What if somebody lives up there?" I said, in desperation. I knew damned well no one lived up that way and hadn't for at least a couple of decades.

The car came to a stop halfway up the bluff. A rotted tree lay across what was once the path forward and blocked our way. The tunnel into Dad's past closed up. He put the car into reverse. I nervously examined the edge. A fall of about twenty feet if the tires went too far to the right.

Dad backed down the drive and continued to talk about how poor Barbara's family was. He explained they lived at the top of that bluff in a log cabin that didn't have any chinking and even in the winter it was left open to the elements. You could look right outside between the logs and see the snow.

We sat at the bottom of the drive, which led to Barbara's old cabin, for a few minutes as Dad continued to tell the story. Barbara's dad was a dirt farmer. Other than those green beans, he couldn't grow much of anything else to eat. The real money was in the hay he grew and harvested, but that only provided enough resources to get them through the winter. Barbara's family was as poor as the dirt on their farm. But Dad loved it there. It was an escape from moments at home. Dad said he loved how the sun used to set over those hills and bluffs. It was a beautiful sight that spat out orange glows so bright it scattered through trees and would leave everything in its wake radiating. He said this theatre of laser lights would last for only a few minutes before everything slowly dimmed, retracted for another day, and moved to dusk and then to darkness. It was this time of evening that sent the searchers out into the night to find the things that were absent from their lives during the day. For some that was rolling the dice, for others, like Dad, it was escaping off to Barbara's. For my grandfather it was the drink.

At the Rock Fair Tavern, Harrison Jamison wandered in, slid up to the bar, and stayed until closing time. Each night he would order Stag beers and tell the bartender to keep them coming. After putting in hours at the grocery store he owned on Main Street in downtown Steelville, he wanted to end his day with a good nightcap. His requests to the bartender often led to seven or eight and never going home. Grandma Charlotte would wait by the door in their little house at the top of Cuba Hill for her husband who, year after year, made it home less and less. As each year passed, she stopped crying when he didn't come through the door. She stopped waiting and went to bed. She'd exchange words with him when he'd stumble through the threshold early in the morning, or when she'd have to knock on the window of his car to let him know it was time to get cleaned up for work. So for Dad, Barbara's cabin, with its chinking missing on the top of that bluff, was a place of security.

I could see and hear how important it was for him to travel down memory lane, despite how grown over it may have been. Coming to a place time had forgotten reminded me that my distressed leather, hand-stitched safari travel bag didn't hold much stock. Though I did wonder how much a copperhead-skin bag would go for in these parts.

Out of the corner of my eye I noticed the reddish brown swirl had reemerged off to the south. It created, once again, a veil over land and sky, and it headed toward us like a fast-approaching storm. My window, now cracked, allowed in the whooshing and popping sounds of tires on dirt and stone.

We sat in a moment of silence as if we had done something wrong and tried our best not to get caught. A dually truck slowed as it passed by where we sat; partially hidden by trees along the bottom of the drive but still visible. The ass-end of our car stuck out over the threshold into the dirt road. Dad looked into the rearview mirror and waved, even though I was certain the driver couldn't see inside from the film over our windows.

I cleared my throat and broke the silence. "We should probably move on, I mean, this could be private property. We definitely look like we don't belong."

The truth was, Dad could pass and did look like he belonged there. I did not. It wasn't only my camel-brown leather flip-flops, matching day bag, and four-inch inseam chino shorts that gave me away. It was my inflections. The sass in my walk. I was a queer, and I had a feeling that if I let my voice shine too loudly outside of our car, I would no longer be in a safe space. I'd let myself believe that people from this part of the country harmed people like me. And maybe that fear was justified? The kids from Cowan had showed me this truth, and Dad had shown me as well.

Dad pointed out the window. "Just up the road there is my old church I want to show you."

We backed the rest of the way into the dirt road and turned to head south even deeper into the maze of country that lay ahead. I looked off to my right to see the field where Dad baled hay and was chased out by snakes, and I thought of Barbara and wondered where she might be today. At the end of the drive, I never asked why he and Barbara broke up or what happened to her. I started to ask when I noticed the dually barreled in at a high rate of speed from behind. It had begun to tailgate us. Dad pulled off to see what they wanted. I closed my eyes, took a deep breath, and reminded myself to be quiet; not to let my gay voice out.

The truck pulled up next to us. Dad rolled down his window and the guy did the same but on his passenger's side. He stared us down and we looked back, not saying a word. I noticed he was about my age but seemed years older in a way that people do when life has thrown some rocks, and maybe a ton of kids, at you. He was handsome, short sandy blonde hair with a stocky build and structured jawline. He asked us what business we had in these parts. Dad said he was from around here and had come back for his fifty-five year class reunion. "Just showing my son around my old stomping grounds." Dad offered his best effort at a congenial grin. The guy looked back at us suspiciously.

"Hey, is the Mount Olive Baptist Church up the road?" Dad asked.

The guy cracked a smile and nodded. "Yeah, it's less than a mile up that way, around the next bend. I can drive you up there if you want to follow."

We agreed and I exhaled. He led the way to the church and honked and waved as we pulled off into a gravel lot. He did a three-point turn alongside us and then he was gone.

Mount Olive Baptist Church stood before us through the haze; its sign warped and worn with weathered wood showing through where white paint once had been. The black, hand-written service offerings across the sign were freshly whited out.

I stepped out of the car and made my way toward the church through the lawn and dusty wind; dead grass crunched below my flip-flops.

"Better watch for those copperheads," Dad called out.

I took a deep breath and closed my eyes. I tried to take in the elements of my surroundings, but my mind took me back to my parents' family room in Cowan and to the drawer of the end-table where Dad kept his Bible. I opened the drawer, wafts of musty old pages released into the air, and I pulled it out to thumb through the title pages that housed ancient maps of Mesopotamia. Inside these pages, over the top of what is now present-day Iraq, was a hand-scrawled dedication that read: *Dave Jamison, baptized May 21, 1961, Mount Olive Baptist Church, Missouri.*

The church outside of Cowan we attended when I was young used to take us a few miles up the road to the Mississinewa River where adults waded out into the still-ness of the water until they were waist deep; children stayed behind on the banks with a few peppered into the river only to their ankles. Our preacher, Pastor Lloyd, raised his Bible toward the sky and shouted words of salvation as he took his other hand and dunked parishioners one by one. The gasps for air from those who were newly cleansed from the sins of this world left me eager for the day when I'd be able to step into those waters and walk out a new man.

On our drives home from the Mississinewa I'd asked Dad if his baptism had been the same. Each time he went into great detail about how his church, Mount Olive, had a natural pool of crystal blue water in a creek that ran along-side an old dirt road where their preacher would dunk them.

"Is God there, too, like he is in our river?" I asked.

"God is everywhere."

I opened my eyes to find the early evening summer sun casting beams through the trees and onto Mount Olive Baptist Church. I wanted so badly to feel the presence of God at that moment, but the truth was that I hadn't felt God around me in a long time. I'd felt as abandoned by God's people as much as the poor structure that stood before me. Each hateful word and action thrown my way chipped at the paint of my soul that held in everything I believed religion was supposed to be. There I found myself surrounded not by a congregation of love but by the desires of a group of people who did not want what I was emitting out into *their* world. Like the old, battered sign of Mount Olive, people had let me down.

The first chip started in kindergarten when I met Jacob. The attraction was immediate. And, no, I don't mean *that* kind of attraction. This was an "I like your plastic bunny scissors and the way you color outside of the lines" kind of attraction. Plus, our teacher put our cubby-holes right next to each other, and she sat us at the same wooden table. So it was a bit of a forced connection, but one that grew into a bonded connection over time.

When the late summer heat simmered down into fall, Ms. Gasser laid earthy finger paints before us and asked us to pick a painting partner. Jacob was there and buttoned up the over-sized dress shirt I wore backward to protect my clothes from any splashes. We stood at our easel and dipped our hands into brown paint and high-fived them onto the paper. We washed our hands back-and-forth in a pan of water, dried them on each other's backward dress shirts, giggled, flicked what remained of the water on our fingertips into each other's faces, and then dipped our fingers in oranges and yellows to dot across the brown tips in front of us. Our hands transformed into turkeys right before our eyes.

Jacob's family was rich. The first time he invited me to stay over he taught me how to play *Oregon Trail* on his Apple II, and we finished the night by relaxing in a hot tub in a mirrored room off the back of the house. We took turns running across the room to play more songs on the jukebox; Def Leppard roared through the air as we sunk back in and flexed our gangly-thin arms in the reflection. His dad worked at an auto factory thirty minutes outside of town and sorted parts on an assembly line that were eventually put together with other parts, from other lines, and turned into cars that would be hauled to lots all across the country. In the 1980s, with only a high school diploma, this type of job gave Jacob's family a nearly six-figure income and us, as kids, some of the best nights of our lives.

The first time Jacob stayed at my house, he was silent as he observed the dolls upon my bed. He stared at each one: Rainbow Brite next to Teddy Ruxpin who sat next to My Buddy who strategically lay next to Robert, my adopted Cabbage Patch, all leaned against the next—Pinocchio, Lemon Meringue, Koosa Cat.

"Don't you have any G.I. Joes?" he questioned.

"No," I said. "But my brother does. We can play with those."

He shrugged his shoulders, undecided.

We didn't have an Apple II or a hot tub or a jukebox, so when Jacob was at my house we played with my dolls. He got over me not having any G.I. Joes of my own, and was content with talking in baby voices as his hand held up Koosa Cat and I talked back holding up My Buddy, as long as I was willing to get dirty in the backyard and build forts out of fallen autumn leaves and sticks. So I did. We'd lay low in those forts where we hashed out escape plans and imagined some evil force waited on the outside.

"I'll make a run for it, and you watch my back. Okay?"

And I did. I watched Jacob's back and he watched mine. All through elementary school when the other kids started calling me names, he'd step up and make them stop. Not with his fists but with his presence. He stood by my side to let me know I wasn't alone. We cemented this brotherhood with a stolen pocketknife from his dad and a poke of our thumbs.

Beyond our blood bond, the next intimate thing we could have shared with each other was our faith homes. I'd take Jacob to church with my family, and I'd go to church with his. Jacob gave his life to the Lord when we were eleven, so I followed suit. I wasn't really sure what I was doing. Religion was important to my parents, and it seemed important to Jacob, so one summer afternoon, at vacation Bible School at his church, I went on stage when the preacher called all lost souls to the alter. He promised eternal salvation. He told us if we didn't go we'd end up in Hell if we walked out the door and got hit by a car.

So up we marched to kneel side by side. Jacob, with his hands clinched and eyes closed tightly, prayed for God to take his heart; to live within him forever. I closed mine and repeated his prayer.

Afterward, we were ushered off to different lines behind the stage to get five minutes of one-on-one time with one of the youth counselors. This college-aged guy with a spikey brown mullet and over-sized glasses congratulated me on becoming a child of God. He handed me a leaflet of Bible stories for kids. "Read this each day, and keep saying your prayers."

He stood and pulled me into a hug; my head met his stomach; his hand clutched the back of my head. But I didn't feel any different.

On the car ride home, Jacob talked about Heaven and what it would be like when we die and go to the other side. He dreamt of roads paved of gold and a grand reunion with those who had left the Earth before us. I rolled down the window and focused my attention on the brown and green tracers from the trees that passed us by. Jacob's words were drowned out by the wind that whipped through the car.

That next Sunday I asked Pastor Lloyd from our church if I could get baptized in the Mississinewa. He told me I had to give my heart to God first. I tried to explain that I had, but

I felt like Pastor Lloyd somehow knew I hadn't prayed hard enough; that maybe I wasn't the type of person the church wanted. After all, Pastor Lloyd's sermons had been focused heavily on fire and brimstone, Sodom and Gomorrah—really anti-gay stuff that could have been interpreted millions of different ways—but I was only a kid. What could I have said or done? I was stuck between what I was always taught— that being gay was wrong—and what I knew I was becoming —gay. Pastor Lloyd put his hand on my shoulder and gave a stern look. "Son, you'll know when God's ready for you."

My relationship with Jacob became different after he gave his heart to the Lord. He'd no longer stand up for me when the other kids would call me names, and he spilled my secret and told them I played with dolls. It was as if Christianity had turned him into Judas rather than a saint. Within two years, all I had left of our friendship were memories that had been quickly replaced with the sinister.

One afternoon during 8th grade Science, our teacher left the room to reprimand a student who had shot spit balls at the chalkboard. In this absence of authority, Jacob crept up from behind and slammed my head into a laboratory desk. The polished slate stung my cheek. I lifted my head and the room spun. The other kids looked on and laughed. He grabbed my hair and pulled me back close to his face; his mouth and hot breath next to my ear. "Faggot," he whispered. I told myself, *Don't cry. Don't you dare cry.* I didn't. Later, he slipped me a note in the hall during passing period. "I'm sorry," it read. "Please forgive me?"

And then Christmas Eve 1993 happened. We had this big old tour bus gifted to the church, its long stretch of crushed velvet gray and white seats extended too far to count. All of us youth boarded that bus to do our own tour: singing carols to the area nursing homes. Although I couldn't carry a tune if it were tied to my back, I couldn't wait to visit all of the seniors around town and bring some holiday cheer into their lives as I shouted:

Hark how the bells,
Sweet silver bells,
All seem to say,
Throw cares away . . .

As I took my seat toward the front of the bus, one girl, two years younger, stopped next to my row as she passed into the depths and looked me square in the eyes as she shook her glasses-framed head: "Queer bait."

She continued on past while echoes of laugher surrounded me. I never understood why people called me queer bait. I mean, *I* was the queer. But it hurt nevertheless.

I supposed the final chip was when Jacob told me that people like me won't ever make it to Heaven. And then a few days later, in gym class, he threw a canister of spray deodorant at my head and asked me to suck his dick as he placed his hands around it in a triangle formation.

I wish I would've punched him in his mother-fucking mouth.

Or maybe it was when Dad said, at the height of the AIDS crisis as we sat in the same family room that housed his baptism Bible, that it was God's punishment to the gays for their wicked lifestyle. Pastor Lloyd had preached it at church.

"He's right!" Dad laughed. "Those queers are good for nothing other than sucking golf balls through garden hoses."

I lay in my room at night and cried. I had accepted I was

gay at fourteen, but geography, and culture, hadn't allowed me to say it.

I TURNED to find Dad examining Mount Olive's sign. I wondered if he was reminiscing about his own faith journey. I squeezed his shoulders from behind and asked what got him involved in the church. He turned his head my way with an ornery grin on his face. "It was Barbara. This was her church."

I raised my eyebrows. "What ever happened with Barbara?"

"Well, she met this college boy over in Columbia and I took up interest in her friend, Lila."

Dad turned toward me, put his hands on both of my shoulders, and we stood, eye to eye. He smirked. "That college boy could have her. I enjoyed Lila more, anyway. She was a good Christian girl but liked to have fun, if you know what I mean."

We laughed ourselves into stitches. Lust for a woman led Dad to Christ. No man had ever done that for me and I silently wished between laughter, and this uncomfortable realization, that no man ever would.

I noticed a stream that ran parallel with the dirt road in front of Mount Olive. I composed myself long enough to get out a question. "Is that *the* creek over there? The one where you were baptized?"

He nodded.

We walked, side by side, to the stream of crystal blue. No one else in the world present but Dad and me. I examined the color and the depth, mystified by how a creek could be as blue as the Gulf, lost for a moment in trying to find a sign. My Judeo-Christian roots kicked in: *Surely this means something.* And then my senses came back and I remembered that field runoff can create algal blooms that turn water the color of the sea. People had literally been dunked for years by their preacher into a vat of chemicals.

Explains a lot, I thought.

I turned back to Dad, who now wore a different kind of smile as he stared into the water. He wasn't thinking about the lure of a woman that brought him to God. He was transported back to another place in time. His eyes looked beyond the crystal blue water and peeled back the years to a cold spring day in 1961 where he joined hands with his friends, his new girlfriend Lila, and along with their preacher walked out of that creek as changed men and women. It was in those waters where Dad gained confidence that everything in life is forgivable and attainable as long as you believe. This was, as much as my secular mind wanted to explain it away, sacred ground for many.

I picked up a small rock at the edge of the road. I touched Dad's back with one hand and tossed the rock into the creek with the other. Its splash reverberated and sent ripples outward in patterns of circular perfection that broke apart and collided with the bank and Dad's memories. I had much hurt there, in those memories. The contradictory of it all. A place to wash sins away, depending on the sinner. A place of acceptance, for some. The night he finally learned I was gay, he brought up the Bible. He said it clearly stated that gays will go to Hell, but he told me he didn't believe it. Even with all the AIDS-punishment talk he had thrown out before to condemn other gays, he told me that God loves everyone: "As long as you live your life doing good in the world."

Maybe Mount Olive and rural Missouri had a hand in it all. Maybe what he learned there helped him find acceptance for who I was. But was I brave enough to accept him for who he was?

I moved my hand to Dad's waist and pulled him into a side hug.

"Let's go," Dad said.

ON THE WAY back out to the main road we sat in silence and I kept trying to think of questions to ask, or something witty to say, but my mind was blank.

The future of our country hung in the balance. What I really wanted to do was punch mother-fuckers right in the mouth for freedom. I wanted to be tough like Dad had always tried to teach me. But would my Judeo-Christian roots kick in, too meek to fight back?—to speak up. The collisions of my past and present had me stuck, treading water, waiting for someone to throw me a line.

3

Dad wanted to find the old Babcock School, a one-room school house that closed after World War II had ended; a place where his aunt Bonnie had taught, and a place I visited once before with Dad when I was eleven. He hadn't been back to the Babcock School since, and now, twenty-six years later, he vaguely recalled where it was located.

We turned off the highway onto another dirt road where field gates blocked off entrances to gravel drives that led to private residences. I couldn't help but think that somebody had to be tied up in a shed back in those parts, or someone was making *Walter White style* meth. It didn't help that almost every gate had a black and orange *No Trespassing* sign, and one had two cameras topped off with confederate flags mounted on both of the posts that held the gate in place.

"Dad, are you sure this is the way to the school?"

He shrugged and shot me a look, like *maybe*.

We barreled forward, deeper and deeper away from

civilization. Dad and I in the middle of nowhere swallowed up by a place the outside world had forgotten.

Houses sporadically dotted the countryside and wooded areas. Some of the homes sat close to the road while others were barely visible down their drives. It wasn't hard to think that if the people who lived in these places had known an ivory tower queer like me had been sneaking around, I would've been the one locked up in their shed.

Goddamn, no one would even hear me scream.

Dad studied one of the long drives that led to a house a distance from the road. The drive was not blocked off by a field gate.

"Dad, that isn't possibly the old school."

"I know, but I think they're home."

Rocks popped the underbelly of the car as we made our way down the drive.

There were a thousand reasons why I felt his decision wasn't good and I began to explain every one, but before I knew it we were a few feet from the house. I made a quick scan of the landscape: a heavily wooded back yard with rolling hills; an old metal barn rusted around the bottom; painted hubcaps that hung from trees to serve as makeshift wind chimes.

Well, shit! I've seen Texas Chainsaw Massacre, and I know how it ends.

A minivan with an off-colored crumpled sliding door sat next to us in the drive. Its back window was a piece of plywood.

"We should probably go. I don't think anybody's home," I said.

Dad stared past the house and into the backyard. He

spoke with confidence. "If we just head off that way by foot, the school is less than a mile away."

"Honestly, you can't be suggesting that we walk back there. This is someone's private property."

He continued to stare off into the distance, mumbled to himself, and calculated a plan. I continued to plead with him. I mentioned the risk of copperheads, and how the heat of the day and his age wouldn't be a good mix. And then I saw her. A woman who pulled back the curtain and peeked out at us.

Dad waved toward the house and told me we should go ask about the school.

Shit. Fuck. Damn.

Dad opened his door. A wall of heat fell into the car and broke the comfort of the cabin.

"I'll just wait here if that's okay," I said.

I watched as Dad made his way to the house, and the woman, now at the front door, cracked it open enough to poke her nose through to get a sense of what Dad wanted. As I watched, my cowardice surfaced: embarrassed, scared, uncertain. I wasn't in control of the situation, and I no longer felt like a bona fide adult.

I grabbed my phone and tapped the app for Facebook. If I made a post and no one heard from me again, the coordinates could be traced. *No Internet Connection* stared back.

I looked toward the house to find the woman now on the front porch, arms crossed, with a blank expression on her face. Dad chatted away and used his hands and arms to exaggerate whatever story he shared. Any hint of what the conversation contained was blocked by the glass of the car and a scrambled country song on the radio. Dad turned and pointed and the woman glared my way. I smiled and gave a nod, then turned my attention to the radio and pretended to find a new station. I kept one eye on her.

Before we left Indiana, Dad pulled a machete from underneath his seat and told me it was in case we ran into any crazy backwoods people or needed to cut the head off a copperhead. That seemed a little absurd, but since he grew up there I recognized he must know that both of these situations could likely happen. And I believed it *was* happening.

I reached down and felt under the driver's seat, but my arm couldn't quite reach without having to duck my head below the dashboard and out of site of the woman who now studied me. I continued to play with the radio and decided if I made a phone call that could look non-threatening but would also let someone back home know what Dad had gotten us into. I tapped the green phone button to pull up the dial screen and proceeded to call my husband, Cory. No ring, only dead air. No connection to the outside world.

I tried a text: YOU WILL NOT BELIEVE WHAT MY DAD HAS DONE. *Unable to send* stared back at me.

Fuck!

I made the decision to get out of the car and join Dad on the porch. Maybe if she saw us together, and I could help Dad tell his story, she'd smile and see we're a dad and a son finding our way down memory lane. I bet she'd even invite us in, but I'd have to interject before Dad could say, "Yes," and let her know we appreciated the offer but we must go.

I opened my door slowly in an attempt to not make any sudden commotion. Off in the distance, beyond the house and over toward the rusted metal barn, I saw movement; but the shade from the trees in that area was too heavy and I couldn't make out what it was. I narrowed my focus and saw skin—two exposed arms—a face. A man in brown work pants with boots, a dingy t-shirt, and a black trucker hat carried some type of tool and he was headed right toward the house, toward the porch, and toward my unsuspecting Dad.

I watched from the car, my eyes level with the dashboard as I crouched in the seat. I had only a moment to react.

Honk the horn?

No.

Jump into the driver's seat, start the car, hit the gas, and run this guy over?

No.

Jump into the driver's seat, start the car, and get the hell out of there? Every man for himself?

No.

I didn't do any of those things. Instead, I watched from the safety of the car as he came within inches of Dad. He carefully slid the tool from his right hand to his left, and moved his left arm and the tool behind his back. He said something to Dad that was inaudible from the car, and he extended his right hand as a greeting but wore no smile upon his face.

Dad carried on with some story, a wide-smile on his face, and he continued to use his hands and arms to accentuate the scenes. Much like I had watched the woman, I studied this man.

Can I be brave enough not to be a wimp? Just this once?

Because I thought I would have to actually save Dad.

With my eyes still on this pair of alleged murderers, I

noticed something peculiar: the man started to laugh; and so did the woman. She even unfolded her arms and patted Dad on the shoulder.

Like, what the fuck?

Almost in unison, everyone turned my way and Dad said something I could not make out. He tried again but mouthed in slow motion: *Come on!*

I opened the door and slithered my way out.

Like Dad had said before, the school was less than a mile behind their house. My face crinkled and responded in complete shock and a little disbelief as I walked their way.

"It sure is, sweetie. Right back there," the woman said as she pointed toward the backyard. "I'm Leslie Meadows and this is my husband, Rick."

Both extended their hands and I shook Leslie's first.

"I got a map of this area inside. I can show you two right where that school is," Rick added.

Dad and I looked at one another, and I noticed for the first time on the trip we understood what the other wanted. Dad's eyes said, *I know you don't want to do this, but please. For me?*

Mine said, *No, nuh-uh, nope.*

But instead, my mouth spoke what my eyes would not say. "Sure, we'd love to see that."

Dad's eyes lit up like a child and he nodded in favor. Rick and Leslie led us through their living room and into their kitchen. It was a space that had been lived in, and I observed one too many knick-knacks upon homemade wooden shelves that had heart-shaped cutouts.

"You boys want a beer?" Rick asked in all seriousness, even though Dad was at least 15-20 years older than him.

Dad, who doesn't drink often, blushed—too embarrassed to say no.

"Sure, we'll take a beer," I responded.

Dad's eyes widened.

"Leslie, get these boys a beer. I'm gonna head down to the basement to get that map."

Leslie pulled two Busch beers from the fridge, popped the tops, and sat them down on the table. The cans had a large mouth bass fish on the sides and read: *Catch one, win big!* I hadn't had a Busch beer since college.

"Have a seat if you'd like," Leslie said as she remained standing, her back against the counter in front of the sink.

Dad and I stood in the middle of the kitchen, next to the table. I reached for my beer. "I appreciate the offer, but I prefer to stand."

Standing put us in a less vulnerable position. I made sure my back faced a corner of the kitchen with no entry or exit way so no one could sneak up on me. I also made sure I positioned myself for my eyes to remain on Leslie with easy observation of the basement door that remained open. Dad carried on in conversation with Leslie about the school, its history, and how his aunt taught there during World War II. I didn't add much to the conversation other than slight nods and fake laughs. I was too busy. I watched the basement door and waited for Rick to return. With the door open I could see two shot guns at the top of the steps on the stairway landing, propped up against the wall. Some sort of knife set hung above the guns. *Antique?* Perhaps. *Scary as shit?* Absolutely.

Leslie interjected. "Have y'all had dinner? I can fix a mess of stuff if you'd like."

"We were just about to head over to where we're staying to have dinner. We should get going." I chugged the rest of my beer and placed the empty can on the table.

Leslie walked toward the fridge. "Y'all can at least stay for one more beer."

"Yeah, you boys need another beer." Rick stood at the top of the staircase, map in hand.

As careful as I was not to get caught from behind, I was trapped.

Leslie handed each of us another beer and Rick walked toward the table, unfolded the map, and spread it out across the top, knocking over my empty can. He pulled a pencil from behind his ear and pointed the tip toward the center of the map. The map was old; faded yellow; topographic. The brown contour lines led from the edges in waves to the point where Rick landed the tip of the pencil. Dad and I leaned over Rick's shoulders, stared down at the map, and I could make out where the pencil pointed: *Babcock School.*

Dad cleared his throat. "Wow, does that say 1948 at the bottom?"

"Yep, this is one of those old-timey maps." Rick pointed toward the far end of the kitchen, "An old fella who used to live back over that way gave this to me a long time ago when Leslie and I bought this land."

Dad smiled and shook his head in disbelief.

Rick moved the pencil slightly down the map. "And here is where our house is today. Less than a mile back to that old school. It's still standing. Y'all want to see it?"

I actually did want to go see it.

"There used to be an old drive that was off one of these back roads," Dad pointed toward the same direction in the kitchen where Rick had pointed, "and it took you right to the school."

Rick laughed. "Ain't no way we're getting back there using the old drive. The only way back there is on a four-wheeler." He pointed to me, "I got two of 'em, you can ride with my wife, and you"—he pointed to Dad—"can ride with me. Let's fill up the cooler first. It's a hot one out there and we'll need beer to get us through."

Leslie reached under the counter into a cabinet and pulled out a small cloth cooler and placed six beers inside. She dumped a handful of ice from the dispenser on the freezer over the top of the beers. "Y'all go ahead. It's too hot out there for me."

That left three of us and there were two four-wheelers. A four-wheeler only seats two people which meant we'd have to take both four-wheelers. I wondered who would drive the other one. I couldn't imagine Dad would know how to drive one of those things, and I sure as hell couldn't either.

Rick tossed a key toward me. "Well, son, you can drive your dad back there. I'll go solo."

Shit.

"I don't know how to drive a four-wheeler."

Rick shook his head and laughed. "It ain't that hard. You just turn the key and go."

We followed him to the front porch. Rick reached into the cooler and cracked open a beer. He looked at the two of us and tossed each a new one. I barely caught mine with my one free-ish hand; a half-drunk beer in my other.

Dad handed his back and told Rick he appreciated it but

he's not much of a drinker. Rick took the can and smirked at the offering. "That's okay. More for me."

I chugged what was left of my one beer and asked Rick what I should do with the empty can. He told me to throw it down on the porch and they'd get it later. It felt almost naughty to litter like that, but I did as I was told and it was pretty cathartic.

Dad patted me on the back. "Better let me drive, Joe."

I handed him the key and felt a sense of relief.

Rick turned to us. "On this handle is the start. Just hit this button and then use the other handle for the gas."

Dad nodded, turned the key, hit the start button and then clinched the opposite handle tightly, thrusting us forward and nearly knocking me off the back. I grabbed Dad's shirt, a splash of beer jumped onto my shorts.

"Easy there, boys," Rick shouted.

Dad leaned back and turned his head toward the right. "Better hold on tight."

I chugged my entire beer and threw the can into the yard. Rick's permission to litter had created a monster. I reached around Dad's torso and felt his sweatiness and was a little grossed out. I let go. "I can just hold on to these bars I'm sitting on."

We made our way from Rick and Leslie's wooded back yard. A grown over trail guided the way to the old Babcock School. I thought of the stories Dad had told me about this area. The ones I half-listened to in childhood. Stories about his great-grandfather, Wild Devil Jim Jamison, who canvased these hills with Quantrill and Jesse James. It's where Wild Devil Jim laid eyes on Eliza Morning Star for the first time; the American Indian girl who would eventually become his wife.

I imagined Dad playing back in these woods with James Pershing, the friend who lived down the road from him and one he considered a brother. Dad spent many days and nights with James, traversing the hills and bluffs that lay beyond the town of Steelville, searching for Civil War relics or pretending to be men in the club house they built only for them.

The deeper we traveled down the path, the more it was grown over and impassable. Rick slowed his four-wheeler to a stop. "From here we walk."

I looked ahead at no path but only woods, lots of detritus, and brush.

Are you fucking kidding me?

I then looked down at my camel-brown leather flip-flops and exposed legs that spanned to the bottom of my chino shorts. Rick opened a storage compartment on his four-wheeler and pulled out a can of *OFF! Deep Woods*.

I sprayed my legs and feet, and I handed the can to Dad and he did the same. Dad handed the can back to Rick and as he lifted his one arm out and began to spray, his shirt rose up and exposed a holster and a pistol. I wondered if this is what he had in his hand back at the house when he crept up on Dad. Back when we were still *strangers*. It made sense, given where the holster was on his body, that he slid the gun over to his left hand and put it into the holster rather than hiding it behind his back like I thought he had done with the *tool*. And it crossed my mind that it was quite possible we might still die. I felt like we were getting to know Rick, but Rick *was* a stranger.

And we were two people who had trespassed on his property.

Rick caught me eyeing his pistol. I quickly looked to the ground and noticed next to my feet lay the remains of an armadillo.

"What? This thing?" Rick grabbed onto the holster and shook it. "It's for protection, and to kill these damned possums on a half shell." He kicked at the carcass.

Dad laughed and put his hands on my shoulders, squeezed, and then pulled me back into him as if to let me know I should lighten up. Rick proceeded into the forest and we followed behind. Sweat rolled down our brows and the thorns from wild raspberry bushes tugged at our legs.

It felt like it was hotter than ever and the mugginess weighed heavy on our backs and soaked through our shirts. The shade from the trees didn't help one bit. I looked down at my legs and noticed a stripe of dried blood from one of the thorns. My feet, dirt covered except for two y-shaped lines under the straps of my flip-flops.

Every few yards Dad would remind us to be on the lookout for copperheads. "They blend right in with the ground."

Rick promised beers. "Just a little more ways and we'll be there and we'll have us some beers."

I remained silent and hoped I wouldn't be shot like one of Wild Devil Jim's victims.

When I was a kid, Dad told me that Wild Devil Jim returned to Missouri after a fifteen-year hiatus in Texas from being run out by Colonel William Monks, who had tried to enforce taxes on rebel residents. After several years of bloody battles where Wild Devil Jim and his gang of rebels moved from town to town and shot any man who claimed to be Union or a follower of Monks, fate caught up with them and most of the gang had been captured or killed in public hangings. Wild Devil Jim did what any outlaw on the run in 1867 would have done—he hopped a horse, rode it to Texas, and changed his identity simply by creating a new middle name and a new birth date. There he became a Texas Ranger, an actual law-abiding man who enforced the law; but outlaw blood still pumped through his veins and his old ways of gambling, shooting, and stealing whispered his name. He faked his death, left his family behind, and rode his horse back to Dent County, Missouri, and back to these hills.

Maybe I can find a little of Wild Devil Jim in me? Maybe I can learn to be tougher.

These tales danced in my mind to keep me from the sweaty mess I'd become. My hair paste had melted down my face and left a sheen that could have passed back home as the result of a good chamomile and seaweed chemical peel. We had walked for a quarter of a mile. As much as I thought Busch beer was shit, I really wanted one at that moment.

"Well, there she is boys," Rick said.

The school was freshly painted bright white and had a new, green tin roof. The door to the school was cherry red. Despite the forest growing up, all around and in between everything, it looked like something out of *Better Homes & Gardens*.

"Did somebody paint this school, Rick?" Dad stated the obvious.

"Yep, one of the neighbors who lives down at the bottom of that hill there, about half a mile away, painted it last summer. Put a new roof on it, too." Rick unzipped the cooler, cracked a beer, and tossed one my way. Dad waved off his offering and instead put in a dip of tobacco.

Rick pulled a large folding blade knife from his side pocket and cut a path from where we stood to the door of the school. The area was more grown over than the route we took to get there. Even with a path cut to guide our way, the remnants of raspberry bushes and thistle reached out and scratched our legs.

The lock for the door was nothing more than a sliding wooden latch. No padlock or deadbolt. Inside was nothing but darkness and the dank smell of old wood.

"I should've brought my flashlight. Sorry about that, boys. It's too dark in there for us to go in. The floor isn't steady and there could be snakes."

I pulled my phone from my front pocket and clicked on the flashlight.

"Well, what do you know? You boys watch your step. Some of these boards might give on you."

The inside of the one-room school house was empty except for a small stage at the front and a couple of crushed beer cans on the floor. I shined the light over the cans and could make out a few letters enough for my mind to make out the rest: *Catch one, win big!*

Dark rectangles remained on the walls where the chalk-boards used to reside. Off in the corner was a fairly large hole in the floor boards. I shined the light into the hole and saw dirt that hadn't seen rain in over a hundred years.

Rick stepped my way. "That's where the wood stove used to be. A few years back some antiquers from St. Louis found this school and stripped it of everything."

I looked around the room unimpressed. It was an old, empty structure in the middle of nowhere that time, and most people, except for Dad, Rick, and the guy who painted this thing, had forgotten. Dad and I had gotten lost on back roads with hidden cameras and confederate flags, we ran the risk of getting killed by Rick and Leslie, and now I was nothing more than a dirty, bloody, sweaty mess. And we still hadn't eaten dinner, which was our original plan when we set out from the motel. *All of that for this?*

And then there was Dad. He smiled. His eyes smiled. He'd waited a long time for this moment to come back to the place where his aunt taught, where he was supposed to attend the first grade but the school closed before that happened, and where he last stood with his mother who has now been gone a long time. A place where he and James Pershing chased each other through the woods and became brothers.

"Well, boys, we should probably head back to the house. It's gonna be dark before we know it."

Dad put his arm around my shoulders and I didn't pull away even though I could feel his sweatiness on the back of my neck. He and Rick swapped deer hunting stories and I even added the only one I knew: the time Dad took me hunting when I was eight, but all I did was talk and he vowed never to take me again because I scared away the deer.

I studied Rick as I told the story. His face solemn like it was when I watched him from the car as he tried to figure out Dad. I wondered if he'd caught on to my gayness and wasn't approving. I'd let my little inflections and hand gestures out with him as I became more comfortable.

Nervous, I darted my eyes to Dad's. He squeezed my shoulder and we doubled over in laughter.

Rick said there were two beers left and he'd like for Dad and me to have them on the trek back. Dad spit out his dip of tobacco and accepted the offering. I caught the beer thrown my way. Dad leaned his head into mine, and it was a feeling I hadn't felt with him since the day he found the letter from my first boyfriend, Steve, and realized I was gay.

I met Steve at college orientation. He was an athlete: tall, brawny, and really funny. We gathered with other orientation groups, hundreds of students, to play a game called *Cross the Line*. It worked like this: everyone started out on one side of the room and a series of questions and statements were made, and if you agreed you went to the other side of the room; if you disagreed you stayed put. Then a discussion would ensue. The idea was to break comfort zones and begin conversations that would bridge our differences. The questions started out fairly easy and then got harder:

If you like Coke, go to the other side of the room. If you like Pepsi, stay where you are.

If you have dealt with divorce in your family, go to the other side of the room.

And then this question:

If you feel like it is okay for people to be gay, go to the other side of the room. If you feel like it's wrong, stay put.

I started toward the "it's okay" side, and suddenly realized no one else was headed that way. I stopped in the middle of the room, looked back at all of my gay-is-wrong-peers, and stared over at the other side where only Steve stood.

"It's okay to come this way," he whispered.

"I can't," I whispered back, even though I desperately wanted to join him on the other side. Part of that was because of all the eyes on us in the room, but the other part was because of Dad.

If I were to admit I was gay, how would that make him feel? As much as Dad encouraged me to be my own person, his words also held me back. The little things that, for some, might get packed away in boxes and stored forever in the back of their mind, for me, stayed in the forefront with their lids open—a constant reminder of Dad's thoughts on people like me. In the family room where he kept his baptism Bible, Dad talked about God's punishment for the gays. He'd limp his wrist and make some statement about queers being good for nothing.

As I'd gotten older, I'd become worried that I was a disappointment to Dad. I never picked up a basketball, ran track, or hit the courts like he'd hoped. He had let me stand on stages and make theatre my thing, but he made comments here and there about watching out for the other male actors because they might try to turn me. Even though I knew I was one of those queers he despised and so often talked about, I never had the courage to tell him.

When I stood in that room during college orientation, literally stuck in the middle, I knew crossing that line would be a public statement and there'd be no turning back. There's freedom in admitting the truth, but when it came down to it I wasn't brave enough to move any farther. So there I stayed, cemented to the in between. I looked at Steve and saw disappointment in his eyes; but I also felt a sense of comfort in his gaze because he understood. For the first time in my life, someone else understood what it was like to live in this skin.

The remainder of the summer before college started that fall, Steve and I exchanged letters through the mail. I'd get one from him and immediately write back—slapping on the $0.32 stamp, and then anxiously wait for three or four days for his return letter. This back and forth went on for several weeks. Then before I left for college, I came home to find the mail on the kitchen table, right where Dad or Mom would always leave it. I thumbed through and didn't find a letter from Steve even though, by my calculations, I should have had one from him. I looked from the kitchen down into the family room and saw Dad reading the newspaper in his easy chair. We had the house all to ourselves. Mom was at her second job selling pantsuits to petite women at a store that sat off the Interstate. I shouted out a quick hello and then hit the stairs up to my room where I found a letter from Steve, opened, on my bed.

I snatched up the letter and began to read it and my stomach cramped with each line that discussed how much he couldn't wait until school started so we could be together; and how much he couldn't wait to kiss my million-dollar smile; and then it was signed with a heart. There was no way this letter could be covered up as a note between two buddies, and Dad had read every line. I felt terror and excitement pump through my veins and flow to my feet. Was it a chance to be free or would I be shunned? I wanted to run.

I folded up the letter, stuck it in my back pocket, and headed down the stairs toward the front door. I had no idea where I was going, but I didn't want to face Dad. As I hit the bottom of the stairs he called to me from the family room. I heard him get out of his chair and head my way. I stood at the front door, frozen in place, and Dad stood opposite of me. *Strangers.* He raised his eyebrows for a moment and then allowed his face to sink into crumpled confusion. A dad and his son, for the first time truly cemented as worlds apart.

"I'm sorry," I said. I didn't know what else to say.

I opened the door and hurried across the yard to my car parked at the end of the drive. I fumbled with the keys, and once they found their way into the ignition I drove around Cowan that entire afternoon and evening. I blared music that disappeared out the downed windows into the corn-fields that swayed in the wind. Being alone on those country roads made me feel like I was the only person in the world. And I was okay with that for a bit. Going back would mean walking into a life that would never be the same. There would always be the before-the-letter and after-the-letter moments.

I pulled over at the elementary school and climbed into the castle on the playground. Next to being on the stage, the castle was my safe space. As a kid, while all the other boys played kickball during recess, I'd hide away in the castle with the girls.

I slid Steve's letter out of my back pocket and unfolded it. I stared at the heart he'd used in place of a formal closing and wished it would go away. I thought maybe I could live out the rest of my life in that castle. I could stock up on food from the fields that surrounded the school and maybe dig a hole near the playground to store it for winter. When school was in session during the day, I could go away but come back at night to eat and sleep. But I also didn't want to miss college, and I wanted to see Steve again. And let's be real, I would've never made it as a homeless man living in a playground castle.

The sun eventually set beyond the fields, and the night sounds of cicadas and crickets rose up from them and told me it was time to go home.

When I arrived, Dad still sat in his easy chair and flipped through channels on the TV. Mom was still at her second job, and we still had the house all to ourselves. I kept my eyes to the ground as I entered the family room and plopped down on the couch. We sat for a moment without speaking, the only sound from a rerun of *Roseanne*. I pretended to watch and let out a fake laugh. I started to think maybe I was wrong. Maybe he wouldn't ask about the letter, and there wouldn't have to be the before and after moments. Then he clicked the remote to flip off the TV. The same nervous surge I felt when I stood on a stage for the first time tickled my stomach and reached into my chest. Dad got up and walked toward me. I closed my eyes and waited for a punch in the mouth. He'd never hit me before, but he'd always talked about punching mother-fuckers right in the mouth. I thought maybe this would've been the moment for him to view me not as his son, but as an enemy that needed to be taken down.

I squeezed my eyes tightly and tucked my hands under my knees to brace myself, but instead I felt the couch sink next to me and Dad's hand on my knee. I opened my eyes and felt the spotlight of Dad's gaze shining into them. I told myself, *No tears, don't let the stinging pain show.* We met eye to eye. *Connected* but *strangers*. I had become what I thought no dad wanted of their son: a limp-wristed queer.

He smiled and squeezed my knee. "Is this a phase?"

"No," I said.

"Welp, I guess I figured as much."

The years of clues strung together in the back of his mind. The dolls, the theatre, all my friends who were girls but *not* girlfriends, and now the letter.

He brought up the Bible. And Hell. But told me he didn't believe I'd go there as long as I did good in this world. He pulled my hand from under my knee and held it. He leaned into me and touched my forehead with his and told me he loved me. I nodded my head in agreement and the spotlight was too bright, it seared right through my eyes, and released the tears. I let go of Dad's hand and didn't tell him I loved him. Instead, I told him I needed to go lie down.

He had given permission to be me. I guess I expected defiance so much that I craved it. I was brave enough to go through so many trends, to be so many things, to leave little clues; but when it came down to it, I wasn't brave enough to allow Dad, the bravest, most macho man I knew, to accept me. Someday, I imagined, it'd all change as the reality set in more and more of who I was. Like, the first time I'd bring a guy home for the holidays, maybe sitting hand-in-hand with him on the same couch, or when we'd go to sleep in the same bed at night. All the things that would happen hereafter might be too much for Dad. Maybe he'd retract his love. I decided that night that separating myself from his grip —*from his love*—would be the easiest in the end, because nothing ever turns out to be a happy story.

BACK AT THE HOUSE, Leslie sat in a swing with a young man, late-teens, who looked more like Leslie than Rick. Rick leaned down, gave Leslie a kiss, and gave the young man a noogie. He squealed, laughed, and pulled away in embarrassment, the way boys do with their fathers when they're just coming of age and trying to figure out the space that separates kid from adult.

"This here is Silas. Our boy," Leslie said.

"He's a real little shit, too," Rick added with a laugh. "You just get home from work?"

I extended my hand and shook Silas's. Dad followed suit and went on to explain to Silas and Leslie the adventure we had on our way back to the Babcock School. Silas listened with an expression on his face that said: *Who in the hell?*

Rick helped Leslie out of the swing. "You boys ready for some more beer?"

Leslie went into the house and the rest of us moved to the picnic table that sat at the other end of the porch. I thought for a moment that Leslie would bring us out dinner with the beers as well, but that didn't happen and I wasn't going to ask. Beer would be our dinner.

"This has to be the last one for me, Rick. I have to drive," Dad said.

Rick raised his eyebrows. "Don't rush off so soon!"

"Oh, we ain't. I'll just stick with this here." Dad tapped his can of dip against his palm.

The evening turned to night. I lost count of how many beers Rick slid my way.

Dad delighted in a captive audience. He shared all his

tried and true stories from the glory days that had brought him back to Cuba—about playing basketball for Steelville High and how he'd refused to sign the dotted line for the track scholarship to Southeast Missouri State.

Silas and I pulled our attention away from everyone else and had our own side conversation. He told me he had been out of high school for a little over a year and he took a job in St. Louis. His commute was eight-five miles one way. It was the only place to get a decent paying job that helped cover college where he was studying to be a nurse. That's the reality of rural life. If one wants to stay close to family while getting ahead, a long commute is the answer. Jobs are every-thing, and people would drive an hour-and-a-half if it provided an opportunity to change the trajectory of their families.

Much of my life I could see in Silas's story. My husband, Cory, in the medical field. My office, a ninety-minute commute one way. Silas was in a small town in the middle of nowhere, and one of the first in his family, like me, to go on to college. Only minor differences in our stories, mainly eighteen years that separated a life I'd lived and the one he had ahead of him. And he's straight. That was kind of a big difference, I guessed.

He mentioned a girlfriend, but I kept silent about Cory. I'm not embarrassed about who I am anymore, and I don't try to hide my life tucked away within letters buried in back pockets, but I am cautious about providing too many details in situations where I'm still uncertain how folks may react. I'd lived the past twenty years of my life in a world where it's okay to be me, but that world also taught me that people like Rick, Leslie, Silas, and even Dad—rural folks—are full of anger and fear.

But I'm afraid of them . . . of what they represented.

I had long been embarrassed by *my* people. These people. I learned long ago to code switch, to live in between my two worlds of highbrows and lowbrows by the language I chose and the way I presented myself; but I also chose long ago to be perceived as one who was better than the lowbrow world—someone who was experienced in worldly things.

Although when Silas talked about how in love he was with his girl, I couldn't help but compare, at least in my mind, the similarities with how my life was with Cory. Not many people in my life understood my commute, or what it was like to have dinner with a husband who discussed operating room bleed-outs while I tried to scarf down a burrito with red sauce. But Silas could. His girl didn't like when he talked about dissections over dinner, either. We laughed. I wanted to tell him about Cory and our similar conversations; but I still feared these people. But these were people like Dad, and maybe people like I would've become had I not been born gay with innate bougie taste. But would they accept me?

Dad, Rick, and Leslie had begun to talk about Donald Trump. Silas rejoined the group conversation and said he hoped Trump would get the nomination because he'd love to cast his first-ever vote for that man. And just like that, our similarities had come to a hard and fast end. I wanted to gag; to tell him how wrong he was and that he was too young to truly understand what was at stake if he voted for Trump. I wanted to tell him that if he spent a few more years commuting to St. Louis, he'd find his way out of this backwoods place and see that there were plenty of opportunities out there that Donald Trump could never provide.

"Yeah," Dad added. "I think he'll bring the jobs back."

They swapped stories of how America used to be, a land of factories that pumped out automobiles and six-figure assembly line jobs—like the one Jacob's Dad had when we were growing up. And they shared their dreams of what they thought it would become under Trump; a place where those factories and jobs would come back. A place where Silas could quit his commute for an assembly line around the corner that had a pension and paid better than a nursing career in St. Louis ever would.

I sat in silence. Outnumbered. Confused. *Maybe these aren't my people.*

Dad and I talked briefly on the drive to Missouri about Trump. He said the engine on his riding mower had acted up and he decided to tinker with it to see if he could figure out what was wrong. "Damn thing was made in China! Last time I'm buying that brand."

He professed all that would change under Trump.

I shook my head, knowing the jobs weren't coming back, and knowing most lawn mower engines, at least in my lifetime, had probably been made in China. I changed the focus over to something more personal. Me. His son. My sexuality.

"But Trump loves the gays!" He had heard him say it on TV. Nothing I added convinced him to think otherwise. So I changed the conversation as I often do when politics come up.

Strangers.

I thought about doing the same with Rick, Leslie, and

Silas, but I didn't. I worried I'd be found out—that I wasn't one of them—but the only one who knew I truly wasn't was Dad, and I didn't think he would give me up even though I was on his turf.

As I listened, what I heard was talk about jobs and the economy. For people in that area of Missouri, and the area where I grew up in Indiana, good jobs aren't easy to come by —at least not without a college degree and, even then, one typically has to move away to make it. I understood that, and I understood that's why Silas made his trek to St. Louis. It's why, in Indiana, I made my trek ninety miles to my office.

I bit my lip and prayed to a God I don't believe in that these people wouldn't be horrible racists. The kind of people who would cheer behind Trump at his rallies when he'd rant about Islamic extremists, Muslim bans, and building a wall to keep out the Mexicans. But there was not one racist word spoken, or even any mention of undocumented workers, Muslims, or refugees. But could there have been underlying racism? Maybe. There had been, only a few houses up the road, confederate flags flying.

Even if not overtly, I wondered if racism had been there. Many white folks haven't examined their own privilege. The writer Ta-Nehisi Coates had said that the rise of Donald Trump was centered on power and privilege—on racism— on convincing the white working class that brown and black folks had taken something from them. And that *something* to many folks was jobs.

I thought about interjecting and raising those ideas around privilege, but I just listened; too afraid of what would be said back to me; too scared I wouldn't know how to appropriately respond. Truthfully, I only listened because of what psychologist Paul Pendler and Phillip Beverley called race-related narcolepsy. The idea that white privilege can be used to "check out" when a person isn't prepared to confront implicit racial bias.

The thing is, reading up on ways to properly examine white privilege, and knowing the appropriate definitions, is a privilege itself. It's reserved for the elite who have the time, education, and wherewithal to do so. Knowledge is power, but knowledge isn't always free. I wondered if Rick and Leslie and Silas, and even Dad, had ever heard of Pendler and Beverly—of Coates—and my guess was they probably hadn't. It was a white, black, and everything in between problem, but it was also a class problem.

Coates also said that the moral arc doesn't bend toward justice like Dr. King promised, it bends toward chaos. He encouraged people to recognize that we all have different arcs, but we must sit with the pain of those whose arcs have tragedy spattered across them. That could have been translated to intersectionality—the collision of race, religion, class, sexuality—but we'd fantasized for far too long and had created our own narratives believed to be real if we only stayed on the surface and didn't dig down deep. There were branches of our family tree that had been covered so thick the base couldn't be seen anymore.

With all of those ideas colliding in my mind, had I experienced race-related narcolepsy with Rick, Leslie, Silas, and Dad? Or was I caught in the cross-fires and silenced by my own knowledge and tattered arc?

The more they talked, the more I reflected on my conversation with Silas and his commute to St. Louis for a job to cover college. I thought about Dad and his lawnmower engine and all his friends who lost their jobs when GM packed up and left town in the middle of the night. I thought about myself: the one who escaped this lifestyle and who sat in judgement with my shiny face and Cartier bracelet. And I began to understand their appeal for Donald Trump. I hate to admit that, it triggers the gag reflex in the back of my throat when I think about it, but I understood their limited point-of-view on what they thought was to come under a Trump presidency. Maybe it had been the beers thinking; too much to process on only a liquid dinner.

I interrupted all their Trump talk and told them it was after 10:00 p.m. "We should probably head back to the motel. We have a big day ahead of us tomorrow."

Dad paused, a look of surprise on his face. Perhaps from the time or that I'd abruptly shut down the conversation.

"Hell, boys, don't rush off so soon." Rick grabbed another beer to slide my way. I waved off the offering with my hand and a smile.

We stood at the table and said our goodbyes, shook hands with Rick and Silas, and leaned in for a hug with Leslie. New friends, though I knew I'd never see them again. I looked at Silas and wished him well, and I really meant it. I hope his life turns out like mine and Cory's. I know what the road ahead could mean for him as he leaves home for a different life in a different town with different perspectives.

I hope he doesn't leave his Dad behind.

Dad and I pulled away and rolled down the windows to let the warm night breeze blow through, silent and content. Even with the headlamps lighting the path forward, I stared out the side into darkness.

4

Smoke filled the bathroom—that, or steam. I couldn't really tell because there was no fan. But the more shampoo I massaged into my hair, the more the smoke appeared. No amount of *Garnier Fructis* could mask the staleness that poured into the cramped space through the vent overhead. On the other side of the wall, I heard a deep voice. I pictured a big, burly man taking a shit, smoking a cigarette, and telling his girlfriend he'd be home as soon as he dropped his load in Kansas City. I towel-dried my back and glanced up at the *No Smoking* sign above the bathroom door.

I slipped on my boxers, pulled open the door, and gasped for the musty fresh air from the room. Dad had awoken while I was in the shower and he sat on the edge of the bed and stared at the TV on full blast. *Fox News.* Aside from the cigarette smoke, my second worst nightmare.

Dad listened intently with wide eyes as if the TV were a hearth and he was a guest at a fireside chat. He made occasional *mms* in agreement. I caught his eye, and he raised one eyebrow with a grin and pointed at the TV. A picture of Donald Trump was on the screen with a voice recording in the background from an earlier call-in to a reporter:

I think the migration has been a horrible thing for Europe. A lot of that was pushed by the EU. I would say that they're better off without it personally, but I'm not making that as a recommendation—just my feeling. I would say that they're better off without it, but I want them to make their own decision.

The image and recording of Trump faded into a young, perky blonde who analyzed his comments on the Brexit vote that took place that day across Britain. Brits rushed to the polls to cast their votes on whether or not they should leave the European Union, something they'd been a part of since it was formed in the early 90s. Though their exit from the Union had been brought up numerous times over the years, it was never taken seriously until a group of nationalist voices talked about sensationalized issues like bringing manufacturing, and more jobs, back to Britain, and too many refugees being allowed into British countries.

Dad leaned back on the bed and rested his body on his elbows. He smirked and shook his head. "He tells it like it is. He gets it."

I hoped Dad's feelings toward Trump had more to do with the economy and less about immigrants. I'd never known Dad to be xenophobic, but perhaps something had emerged from within in the last twenty years. Maybe the loss of manufacturing jobs had created a hatred toward the other. I hadn't thought it when we were back at Rick and Leslie's, but maybe Dad was becoming a rallying Trumpian.

But how do you ask someone if they're a racist, especially your Dad, without ruffling a few feathers? Without putting an end to whatever the trip to our past was supposed to be about?

I looked down at the navy blue carpet and kept my eyes from the TV. *Strangers.* I contemplated these questions, but I also thought about how much my favorite *Orlebar Brown* swim trunks would go up in price since the Brits were leaving the European Union. No more showing off my athletic thighs in those three-inch inseams. I'd never be able to afford another pair again.

IN THE LOBBY, next to the over-stuffed floral couch and love seat, sat the continental breakfast for the motel. Five wooden square tables sat in the same area. I looked the breakfast over: cereal; bread of several varieties; fruit; biscuits and gravy; coffee, juice, and milk to drink.

"Good morning, gentlemen," Rhonda called out from behind her post. "I take it you all had a good night?"

"We sure did!" Dad said. "I took my son back to where I was baptized in Lick Creek and then we went to the old Babcock School."

He went on about our adventures with Rick in the woods. I picked over the breakfast. After a make-your-own whole wheat waffle stand didn't magically appear, I settled on Cheerios and a slice of toasted wheat bread with Nutella. Coffee, black. Dad continued to talk and Rhonda seemed as interested as she had been the afternoon before.

"Is that right? Well, you two have a good day." She disappeared back into an office behind the counter.

Dad put his arm around my shoulders and squeezed tight with a laugh and told me to get the open table closest to the TV while he got his breakfast.

Out of the five options, one table was taken by an older man and woman, years of life creased on their foreheads, and another by a younger family of five—a mom, dad, two teenage daughters, and another daughter who sat on her knees near the table and played with a hand-stitched cloth doll. I nodded my head and said "good morning" to both families and took the open table between their two tables. The TV, closer to the older man and woman than to us, was on no other than Fox News.

Damn, are there any other stations in this town?

I settled, cautious not to spill my coffee. Dad soon followed behind and settled in, plate full of biscuits and gravy.

"Yeah, buddy, let's listen to the rest of what Trump has to say."

Indeed, Trump's image was back on with a voice-over from his presidential-run announcement that had occurred one year earlier:

When do we beat Mexico at the border? They're laughing at us, at our stupidity. And now they are beating us economically. They are not our friend, believe me. But they're killing us economically. The U.S. has become a dumping ground for everybody else's problems. When Mexico sends its people, they're not sending their best. They're not sending you. They're sending people that have lots of problems, and they're bringing those problems with us. They're bringing drugs.

They're bringing crime. They're rapists. And some, I assume, are good people.

I tried to understand what nonsensical drivel I'd heard, as the talking heads discussed whether or not those comments would hurt Trump in the end since he continued to win every single primary held across the country.

"I just love that man," the older woman said as she turned toward our table. "He's got my vote."

Her husband focused his energy on Dad. "My job was outsourced to Mexico after thirty years. Both our kids moved away to California to find good jobs because they don't exist in Wisconsin anymore."

And with that, he pulled Dad in.

The discussion across tables continued much as it had the night before at Rick and Leslie's with talk about GM leaving our hometown and how one could even get a good factory job in Cuba and Steelville back in the day but not anymore. The Wisconsin couple shared similarities. Dad even threw in his lawnmower engine story and how it was made in China.

I wanted to sink down into my seat. I thought about taking my Cheerios and Nutella toast under the table and finishing my breakfast there. At least I could make eye contact with the girl who sat on the floor and we could share similarities, too—eye rolls, I imagined.

I looked over at the family of five. They sat in laugher and spoke Spanish. Their body language was enough for me to know they were not focused on the TV, the words of Donald Trump, or the conversation on our side of the room. They enjoyed breakfast as a family. The dad reached over and tickled one of the daughters on her side as she squealed;

the mom pointed sternly toward one of the other daughter's plates—I'm sure she told her to "finish your food"—and then she patted her daughter on the head with a smile.

I turned back toward Dad and the couple from Wisconsin and cleared my throat to interrupt the conversation. "You say your kids live in California?"

The wife took my bait as Dad and her husband continued their conversation.

"Our daughter lives down in San Diego and our son lives in LA." She beamed. It was easy to see she was proud of her kids.

"I love California. I've been there several times. What do they do?"

"Our daughter is a doctor and our son makes films. Well, he's not big time yet, but he's working on it."

It sounded to me that neither kid had planned to stay in Wisconsin, jobs leaving or not. But who was I to make that assessment out loud?

"What brings you to Cuba, Missouri?" I asked.

Her husband jumped in before she could speak. "When I lost my job, I became a trucker." And then as fast he entered, he exited and continued on in his conversation with Dad. His wife smiled in a way that was hard to distinguish if she was tired of being interrupted by a man but had no energy left in her to point it out, or if she was truly in love with her husband and admired this new life they had created together.

She turned back to me. "We come this way quite often. We always stay here when we do. Isn't this a nice place?"

I looked around at the overstuffed couch and love seat and all of the pastels. Actually, it wasn't that bad. I had to admit, despite assuming the place was overrun with bed bugs and maybe had a body or two stashed away somewhere, it was nice and clean. Well, except for the cigarette smoke that wafted through the bathroom vent. I wondered what kind of shit-holes the two of them had to stay in across the U.S. And then I wondered if they had bed bugs and if bed bugs could crawl fast. Like, from them over to where I sat.

"Yeah, it's really nice, and this breakfast isn't half bad," I said.

My thoughts drifted for a moment to what they would do if I stood up, threw my hot coffee their way, flipped over the table, and screamed, "Wake the fuck up, people. Trump is a lunatic!"

And then I realized I fit in.

If I stayed silent about my political views, they'd never know. I looked like them. If I stayed really quiet and didn't let too much of my gay voice out, I could pass as a straight white male. Dad spoke their language, and I carried on with her like I was trying to develop a new best friend. But I knew any minute she would ask the question I'm so worried people like her will ask: "Do you have a wife?"

Then when I truthfully answer, "Yes, I'm married, but I don't have a wife," that would be the end of our conversation. She and her husband had already shown me enough about their views to know her tiny brain couldn't comprehend who I am. I had bet she would look me over and think, "Mhmm . . . that boy's a queer." Everyone would laugh; throwing confetti and expletives my way. Rhonda would reemerge and jump on the counter doing the *YMCA*.

I snapped out of my daydream.

"Do you get to see your kids often? Are they married?" I continued, knowing I may have opened a can of worms. Dad squeezed my knee under the table.

"We do. John always volunteers to be assigned the loads out west when they come along. Our daughter just got married, and our son, well, he's in a relationship but they're not married yet. I guess, well, it's legal now for them to do so. If you know what I mean."

Her husband, now known as John though he'd not formally introduced himself, stopped the conversation. "Well, Honey, we should get going."

I was so caught up in talking with the wife that I had ignored most of Dad and John's conversation and wasn't quite sure what, about Trump and his ideas, they had discussed. Or how loudly. I looked toward the family of five, seemingly unaware of the environment around them, and I was relieved.

It's probably for the best.

John and his wife, whose name I never caught, gathered up their paper and plastic breakfast dishes and headed toward the trash.

"It was nice meeting you," she smiled.

"Mateo," John called out to the family. "See you on the road."

The father of the family of five, Mateo, stood, an American flag belt buckle on his pants. He walked over to John and shook his hand. "See you back around these parts in a few months."

John nodded. "Adios, hermano."

Mateo sat down again to finish breakfast with his family.

I sat mostly in disbelief. I had crafted a narrative in my head about both families. Apparently, I was wrong.

They have a gay son and they're friends with the Hispanic family. And the Hispanic family probably knows their views on Trump. How is this even possible?

"Well," Dad turned his attention to me. "How about I hit the shower and then we can go on another adventure?"

After the escapade with Rick in the woods searching for that old school, I was willing to see where the day would take us. I had a good time, despite all of the literal blood, sweat, tears, and melted hair paste—which actually had done something positive for my skin.

WE ROLLED into Dad's hometown of Steelville around mid-morning. The community was small and greeted guests with only a few offerings such as a couple of banks and Mom and Pop specialty shops. Side streets darted off in either direction up the hills, mainly landscaped with houses.

Since Dad's time there, Steelville had become known as the "Floating Capital of Missouri" due to *weekenders* who traveled to the area to float down the Meramec with coolers tied to their inner tubes. The community had owned its *tourist town* persona, even though there were no hotels or motels. There were, however, plenty of cabins to rent along the river, and parks for RVs and trailers and such. I felt a little relieved that Dad didn't throw out those options, and I began to understand that our stay at the motel in Cuba was a luxury. I mean, Nutella on toast and an old musty air conditioner was better than roasting wieners over a fire.

"I want to stop into this bank here real quick-like to see my old friend, James Pershing," Dad said as he pulled off of the main road.

Out of the two banks in town, James was the president of this one. Growing up, James and Dad were more than best friends. They were chosen brothers. They raced cars down Main Street together, and, even though they hung a hand-painted old piece of wood on the side on their club house that read: *No Girls Allowed,* they eventually let girls in as they grew older. James and his dad also introduced Dad to the Boy Scouts, and this led Dad to Scoutmaster Earl.

Scoutmaster Earl was a father figure. Someone who taught Dad the hidden rules in life and of boyhood; of what it meant to grow into a man who shows up. He took all the boys in the Troop on weekend excursions where they tied ropes, pitched tents, and told ghost stories by camp fire. They took canoes and floated down the Meramec. Scoutmaster Earl had fought in World War II. On these trips he gathered the boys around, each leaned in and hung from his words, as he told them about his days of fighting Nazis with his bare fists and then related the story to lessons on how to wrestle a bear if a daring adventurer happened to get caught out in the wild. As they grew from *Boys* to *Eagles,* Scoutmaster Earl taught them how to draw back bows, shoot guns, hunt deer, and he showed up each Saturday night for Dad's basketball games. He stood quietly against the wall, observed, and come Monday he gave Dad pointers on how to perfect his jump shots. He talked to the boys about girls and how to treat a lady—to always open doors, and never miss an opportunity to tell them how stunning they are.

67

When Scoutmaster Earl wasn't around, Dad and James relived the adventures he had taught them in the woods and hills outside of Steelville.

But when Dad moved to Indiana to work on the pipeline, he lost touch with James Pershing for some time. James had gone off to college and was busy with his days, nose-deep in a book. His nights were spent chasing the co-eds along sorority row. Dad's days were spent traversing roads between Indiana and Louisiana inspecting valves. At night, Dad scrubbed his hands in a roadside motel sink, while the pink and blue neon *No Vacancy* lights peered through the window and illuminated his face as he washed away the crude stains of the day.

James lavaliered his college girlfriend sophomore year. He fastened the necklace gently from behind and promised that marriage would come for the two of them in three to four years. Dad and Lila broke up when he left for Indiana because the distance proved to be too far. There was no special goodbye. Only a phone call from a payphone outside of a gas station south of Shreveport. Dad continued on with his church ways, met another church girl, and he made her his wife.

Dad and James were worlds apart.

Fifteen years later in the late 1970s, Dad pulled back into Steelville, his marriage failing, and congratulated James on taking over the bank.

"I haven't seen James since that time," Dad said as we entered through the doors.

But that hadn't stopped their friendship and brotherhood. At least in Dad's mind, James still raced cars alongside him and made rules for their club—even if only in his daydreams. James never made time for Dad when he came to town, but they still exchanged Christmas cards each year and somehow, for Dad, that was enough to still consider him his best friend—*his brother*.

Inside the bank, tellers sat at their stations. "May I help you?" one woman called out. Dad continued walking on toward offices off to the side. I smiled and gave a slight wave to the teller and continued to follow closely behind.

"Well, Mary Jane Simmons," Dad called out with a loud laugh as he leaned against the doorway to her office, both arms up and against the frame. I stood behind, tip-toed from side to side as I looked over Dad's shoulders to get a glance of this Mary Jane.

"David Jamison! You don't say. You in town for the reunion?"

Dad and Mary Jane danced around small talk and caught up on who would be at the reunion and who wouldn't; who had died from their class and who'd gotten fat.

"Did you come to see James?"

"Yeah! What is that old fart up to?"

Mary Jane picked up the receiver to her multi-line office phone and hit two buttons, one that put the phone on speaker and another that fast-dialed a number. The phone rang and rang until the beginning of a voicemail started: *You've reached the desk of—*.

Mary Jane hung up the phone.

"Well, he's not answering. It's been a really busy time for him. The Board's in town so he may be in a meeting. Ever since his book launch his calendar fills up fast."

Mary Jane got up from her desk, parted between us, and

walked out to the lobby. She motioned us in her direction and continued to talk. "Let me run upstairs to see if he's available. Just wait down here for a second." She disappeared up a set of stairs.

Dad and I stood in the lobby next to a life-sized cardboard cutout of James that advertised the release of his book. Dad explained that he had heard James had open-heart surgery a few years before, and that he had died on the operating table. His self-published book was about what his time on the other side, with Jesus, was like before he was sent back down to Earth with a new mission to help others find their spiritual path to God.

Jesus Christ. I thought.

"Boy, I'd like to get my hands on this book," Dad said as he picked up an order form that sat on a table next to James's life-sized cutout.

I reflected back on our afternoon before at Mount Olive Church. I had been pained by religion, but the experience next to the crystal blue creek where Dad had been baptized allowed me see how important religion was to him and how much it shaped his life. Even if he had been drawn to it because of a girl, and even though it had created another wedge between the two of us. I looked the life-sized cutout of James up and down but decided to remain open-minded; despite the fact I felt like his book was another propaganda tool to recruit folks into a space that taught *hate* in the guise of *tolerance*.

"I bet we can get one from James." I picked up an order form, too, and wondered how anyone could believe this shit.

Remain open-minded, J.R. Remain open-minded.

Mary Jane's voice rang out from behind us. "Well, James

isn't seeing anyone right now. It's a big, big day for him, but he said to let you know he'll be at the reunion and he'll see you there."

"If we want to get one of these books," I responded, holding up the order form, "do we just leave this with you?"

Mary Jane tilted her head to the side and her eyes lit up. "I'm sure James will have them for sale at the reunion. I bet he'll even sign it for you if you ask."

I put my order form back on the table. Dad looked at me with a big grin on his face, order form still in hand, and he used it to motion me toward the door. He didn't show an ounce of sadness for James not stopping his work to give him five minutes of his time. He had grown used to their separation, but wouldn't allow before and after moments for the two of them to exist. I understood this, and Dad's lifelong search for a brother.

Out of my two brothers, one was fifteen when I was born and the other seven. Neither of them brothers to one another, but both of them half-brothers of mine. Over the years, they'd shift from one family to the other. One disagreement with his mom and Dad's son would come stay with us for a few weeks, and Mom's son would go stay with his dad when the same would happen.

My oldest brother was gone by the time I was three, off to the Navy and then on to a vagabonding life living from state to state and couch to couch. He didn't come home much, and when he did there wasn't time for his little bro. One of my only memories of him being a brother to me is when I was seven. He had come home for a few days' break from the Navy and asked to stay with Dad and Mom. Since our home wasn't his main stay, he didn't have a room. He stayed in mine for that week and slept in my twin bed as I lay on a pallet of blankets on the floor next to him; my heart beat fast, overstimulated by his return. In the darkness I tried to make out the bumps in the popcorn ceiling and count them to fall asleep, and I listened to him snore and wondered if he'd ever come back again.

The day he left, he slid his black canvas wallet from his back pocket and flipped it open. He pulled out a card for a tanning salon and handed it to me. "Go here when you get older. Chicks love a guy with a tan."

I stared at the logo, a foil-printed green palm tree engulfed by a bright yellow sun. I moved my thumb across the image and dreamt of a future J.R. surrounded by women in bikinis drinking Piña Coladas in a hot tub. It was the 80s, and I imagined the future would always be like 1986 with bright neon geometrical patterns floating in the background. I kept that tanning salon card in the closet with all my toys for years. It eventually found its way into my own wallet until one fall day, sophomore year of college, I threw it in the trash. I had already come out and decided I didn't really need the card anymore. I hadn't spoken to my brother in years and trying to attract girls in bikinis wasn't really my thing.

Dad told me once that my older brother doesn't come around because he blames him for the troubles he's had in life. He told him if it hadn't been for the divorce and Dad moving on to another life with another son, maybe his life would have turned out differently. Maybe he would've stayed in town. Maybe he would've called Dad each Father's Day, or stopped by with his family to have dinner on Sundays while Dad passed on the advice he learned all those years before from Scoutmaster Earl. But none of those things were to come.

I carried the guilt of being born and shifting the lives of everyone else. I'd spent a lifetime trying to make up for something that was no fault of my own, and I'd done that by trying to bridge the gap between these two worlds. But let me tell you, it's really fucking difficult to always play the martyr.

My other brother and I were closer for a few years. Being only seven years older than me, he was around and we spent most of my childhood in disagreement; I guess like young brothers should. We did live in the same house since we shared the same mom. There are many Christmas photos in front of the fireplace where he and I wear the same outfit, standing side-by-side; an ornery grin on my face, a frown on his. He liked to be his own person, and wearing a maroon and black stripped pull over when you're twelve—to match your five-year-old brother—does not scream independence. But he, too, left at eighteen for the Navy; except when he came home on visits during his time in, he was a brother.

I grew into a teen and he talked to me about brotherly things. He introduced me to classic rock and roll. These little subtleties were a changing wind from the time I was a kid and he put the Mötley Crüe tape into the back of Teddy Ruxpin, and I had nightmares for weeks of Teddy singing *Shout at the Devil*. He talked to me about the meaning behind songs from bands like *Crosby, Stills, Nash, and Young*, and we drove his black 1984 Camaro over hills on country roads, bellies tingled from the sudden lift and drop, while he showed me how to properly inhale a cigarette. He talked to me about girls, and he told me to wrap it up and make sure I didn't get anybody pregnant. I mustered my way through those conversations and pretended to understand what he meant, as I French inhaled my smoke knowing damned well I wasn't ever going down that path. And then it all changed.

Not long after college started and Steve and I had begun to date, my brother and I went on one of those long drives and found ourselves lying on our backs in the grassy area in the middle of the track at Cowan High School. We stared at the stars and guessed at constellations, and he asked me how life was treating me with the college girls. There was a pause in the conversation before I told him I was in love. "Steve's his name," I said. And after I said it, there was no going back. No *just kiddings*. I couldn't be like, "Never mind!"

He grimaced. "You are? But what if people think *I'm* gay?"

We never went on anymore long drives after that.

Even though he has since come around, those memories of the before and after moments still danced in the back of my mind; hanging around to remind me that there is a fine line between rejection and acceptance.

The straight men in my life always leave. I spent years after that night in Cowan searching for someone else to be like a brother. Someone who would take all of me in without exception. There was Lucas and Chris and Chase, but eventually they got girlfriends, married, started their own families and that brotherly closeness was gone. I never found my James quite like Dad had, even if their friendship really only existed in his memories; a place curated so perfectly where there are no before and after moments.

5

Ever since Dad retired in 2004 from his days of working on valves, he's been obsessed with genealogy. It makes up his days and his nights. In fact, when Cory and I bought our house in the summer of 2005, all of the plumbing had to be replaced because the home had sat empty for two years and was not winterized—we got a heck of a deal on it, though, but that's another story—and I asked Dad if he would get under the house and change out the pipes. He wouldn't do it. He had been retired *one year* and *one month*.

The truth was, Dad didn't want to take time away from his genealogical research. It had become his full-time job in retirement. Once Mom introduced him to a computer—yes in 2004—he went wild. A search here and a search there, hours on Ancestry.com, and print out after print out of people who were likely our great-great-this and our great-great-that. There were connections that ultimately did not connect, like that we may be heirs to the Anheuser-Busch Company. Come to find out, one of our ancestors worked there in the early days of operation and was friends with Eberhard and Adolphus, the founders.

And then there were the stories that were confirmed to be true. Like stories Dad had heard from his great-grandmother, Eliza Morning Star, about his great-grandfather being a Missouri outlaw that were solidified with a stroke of a key and connection to the World Wide Web.

Wild Devil Jim Jamison. A leader in Quantrill's Raiders. A Bushwhacker. A member of Jesse James' Gang. My great-great-grandfather.

It's almost hard to believe that could be true. I wonder what he would think of his great-great-grandson being a liberal queer. A guy who doesn't even own a gun. Wild Devil Jim withstood fourteen bullet holes in his time, and it's well documented that he rode into several towns in Missouri and Kansas and killed all the men who claimed to be Union, shot by shot. He was one mean son-of-a-bitch. God rest his mother, Sarah Jamison's, soul.

One thing Dad uncovered in his research was that Wild Devil Jim lived two lives and had two wives: one in Texas with whom he had no children, and another in Missouri, Eliza Morning Star, who is my great-great grandmother. In some accounts, he's James Alexander and in others James Lane. It had long been speculated he faked his death in Texas to finish out his life in Missouri. The mysteries that surround the records of Wild Devil Jim are as disrupted as his checkered past. But family stories get passed down, and there was much Dad already knew about who created each little piece of his DNA. Those who made him brave. Those who made his temperament half bad decisions and half loyal and loving. Eliza Morning Star told her great-grandson stories about growing up on a dirt farm outside of St. James and how her parents hid outlaws to earn money to get them through the harsh winter months. Dad listened intently, took in each word, and seared these images into his mind; saving them for stories he would one day pass on to his own son.

In 1876, Jesse James had taken a short, three-year break from outlawing after the Younger brothers—a couple of badass bandits who he often rode with—were arrested; but simple family life was not for him and he brought back together some of the men from the old gang to start a raid across Missouri and the upper-Midwest. Wild Devil Jim met Jesse and Frank James almost two decades before when they rode side-by-side as members of Quantrill's Raiders, and they were more than happy to add him as an honorary member of their new gang. Half of Missouri saw these men as bandits and the other half saw them as heroes. *The Robin Hoods* of their time who took from the rich and gave to the poor. Since half saw them as bandits, they had to rely on the other half to hide them out and many of the former Cherokee families, whose fathers and mothers had left the Trail of Tears to begin new lives with new names in Dent County, were the poorest of the poor and took them in on trade for cash, gold coins, and jewels. One of those families was Frances Asa Eagle and Mary, my great-great-great grandparents.

In the days of Quantrill, they broke bread with the gang members over candle light, lifted floor boards in the sitting room to usher the men into hiding, and lowered bags of stolen coins into their well. When the law became too heavy in the area, they guided the men into the night to a hole in the side of a foothill that fed into a cavern system. They were loyal, and that's why Jesse's new gang, along with Wild Devil Jim, returned to Frances Asa Eagle and Mary more than a decade-and-a-half later when they sought refuge, once again, from their outlaw ways.

When the men returned, Frances Asa Eagle and Mary had begun a family; but this didn't stop them from welcoming them back. In fact, the kids provided more hands to help with the hiding. Their 10-year-old daughter, Eliza Morning Star, was given the task by her mother to be the launderer. The men would at times be gone for days, riding into nearby towns to hold up banks or slipping into the back country to road agent a train. During their rest days on Frances Asa Eagle and Mary's farm, Eliza Morning Star gathered up the men's dusty clothes and scrubbed them back and forth on the washboard. Reddish brown splashes from the muddy water dotted her arms and face and dried quickly in the mid-morning summer sun. She repeated the process in an adjacent barrel full of fresh water from the well, and then she pinned the clothes along a wire that was hidden from sight, tucked away between the chicken coop and a grouping of white oaks. In the evenings, before the men retired for the night in their safe space under the sitting room boards, Mary ladled bean soup with venison into bowls from the cast-iron pot that hung in the stone hearth behind the house. She handed each bowl to Eliza Morning Star, who carried them into the house and placed them in front of the men.

For the next year, these daily and evening rituals were common place on the farm. But as the year rolled on, Wild Devil Jim passed on opportunities to head out with the gang and stayed behind to help Frances Asa Eagle raise sheds and nurture crops that yearned for a tending through the dust. The Governor of Missouri, Thomas T. Crittenden, was hot on their trail and had put up reward money for the gang's capture—dead or alive. Day by day, and one by one, the men were arrested, fled the gang to create new identities in some far off town, were killed, or surrendered to authorities. Each message of these happenings, which was brought to the table during dinner-time conversations, kept Wild Devil Jim on the farm and caused Frances Asa Eagle's welcome to the other men to wear out. That spring, as the remaining members of the gang found new places to hide, Jesse James tested his luck and rented an apartment in St. Joseph, Missouri. With a high reward out on his head, most assumed he would be taken down by his landlord or a neighbor. Instead, he was shot and killed by Bob Ford, a member of the gang.

Wild Devil Jim's outlawing days were over. He stayed at Frances Asa Eagle and Mary's farm for the next four years. Each spring, he planted seeds in the dust, and in the summers he tended to the sheds and chased the chickens across the yard. And in the fall, he helped with the harvest and hunted deer to feed the family through the winter. Each year Eliza Morning Star got a little older, and by age fourteen Frances Asa Eagle and Mary offered their daughter over in marriage to Wild Devil Jim. He was thirty years her senior. This wasn't uncommon at the time, though. Most young women left the home between the ages of thirteen and fifteen to start their own families. The average life expectancy at the time was forty. Wild Devil Jim had surpassed that, and Eliza Morning Star's was thought to be a third over. Even still, as Dad has shared this part of our family's history with me over the years, I often questioned if a fourteen-year-old could make a life-altering decision that would change the trajectory of her life. I mean, when I was fourteen I still played with dolls, and when I had some down time I tried to learn the latest moves from *Yo! MTV Raps*. Listen, I never underestimated the opportunity to become popular at a middle-school dance held in the Cowan Junior High cafeteria.

But when her parents offered her up in marriage, did she go willingly? Without kicking and screaming? It was the 1880s, and life was different then. I've never had to fetch water from a well or hide bandits in the confines of my crawl space. And at fourteen, unless something horrific occurred, my life wasn't considered a third over.

It's unclear if Eliza Morning Star saw Frances Asa Eagle and Mary ever again. She and Wild Devil Jim settled down in Sligo, and there aren't family stories about happy endings where they went back each weekend and helped on the farm or caught up in the kitchen as Mary ladled bean soup and Eliza Morning Star placed the bowls neatly on the table. Instead, Eliza Morning Star bore eight children for Wild Devil Jim. She cooked their meals each day, scrubbed their clothes on the washboard next to the house; reddish-brown spots splashed on her arms and dried in the mid-morning summer sun. As the kids grew older, they began to help with the chores until they made their own ways with their own families.

Wild Devil Jim grew distant. He became a man of few words who left the house in the mornings to be gone until the evenings, and no one knew where he had been. His tall, lanky frame moved across the yard to take a rest on the steps to the porch; his steel-gray eyes stared through any questions anyone would ask, so people stopped asking. But they knew of his past. They knew of his wife. He wasn't given the nickname Wild Devil Jim without reason, and the stories from his past that earned him the name gave him many privileges. And by association, those privileges were extended to Eliza Morning Star. Just as her father was able to pass his wife off as full Cherokee—even though there were whispers about the darker color of her skin being something other than Native—Wild Devil Jim passed his wife off as white by the same accounts.

Being the wife of a former outlaw that most of the town was still afraid of provided her with strange protection and privileges not offered to others who looked like her. She could pass, but her husband helped her pass more. There's complexity in this type of privilege. On one hand, there's bravery in doing what one wants to do and not being held back because of looks—what's on the surface—and on the other hand there's a deep sadness when these types of privileges force people to run from who they are. Is it bravery or cowardice? Perhaps a bit of both. Modern day philosopher Kwame Anthony Appiah has said, "Race is fiction but racism is not."

I imagine the town folks in Sligo whispered as Eliza Morning Star shopped along Main Street for the latest inventions that made raising a family easier, with her tawny skin glistening in the sun. She probably smiled at them with a nod and kept on walking. She held her head up high. In some ways, I imagine it was her raising a finger to *the man*. A *fuck you* to say I can go where I please when I please. But perhaps holding her head up high was to hide the hurt underneath; she was forced to cover up who she was by burying her past under layers of skin. That past was always there, trying to inch its way to the surface, but willpower and a smile kept it at bay.

Wild Devil Jim died in 1925 at eighty three years old. After surviving fourteen bullet holes during his life and escaping from the gallows of the law, pneumonia got the best of him and he went peacefully at home. All of their kids had come of age and married and moved to different parts of Missouri. Some stayed nearby, and others moved to the big city. Eliza Morning Star left Sligo and went to St. Louis to live with a daughter. She stayed there for the next twenty-five years until she outlived her, and then she made her way back to central Missouri to live out the rest of her days with her grandson and his family in Steelville.

When she moved in with Dad's parents, Eliza Morning Star was nearly eighty years old. She sat in the backyard, the long braid of her silver hair hung over her shoulder and touched a knee while she shucked corn from the garden or whittled her own walking sticks out of fallen branches. Her skin, still tawny but bronzed more by the sun, wrinkled around her amber eyes. Dad snuck up behind her and tickled at her ear with a long blade of grass. She swatted behind her and yelled, "Davey, I know that's you!" She spoke of her outlaw husband and the havoc he wreaked all over Missouri, and she spoke of her Native roots. She never once spoke of her other roots, and she never once said that she loved or missed Wild Devil Jim.

Dad had heard the rumors over the years. That his great-grandmother carried a secret with her. A rumor that she wasn't fully white, and perhaps not even fully Native. He heard it from a Black man he baled hay with who told him they were cousins. He heard it from the kids at school who teased him about the dark-skinned woman who sat in their yard. But he never heard it from her, even though she always told him to be brave.

The one place that may have held the key to unlock it all was the Dent County Courthouse in Salem, Missouri. The place where Wild Devil Jim married Eliza Morning Star and the place where he died, for the second time.

EACH CURVE of the highway to Salem led off into woods so thick that it would be hard to tell what was left or right, or backward or forward, without a compass directing the way. Some of the areas likely hadn't been touched by humans in decades. I imagined Wild Devil Jim riding through the area, alongside a gang of rebels, waiting for the right moment to strike.

The more I tried to stare through the trees, the more they all blended together into a blotch of brown and black. I realized how lost one could get in those woods. I understood how frightening and peaceful that would be. And then I thought about bears and copperheads and the movie *Deliverance,* and I decided I was good. No more mental exploring through those parts for me.

Salem was a little larger than Steelville but nothing more than a forgotten town that no one would stumble upon, unless they had gone out of their way to go off the beaten path. Albeit small, people were out and about in herds and greeted each other with smiles and waves. Nothing else to do, I supposed, except walk around town. I was a little jealous of how easy and simple life seemed. Back home, most people were glued to their phones and cringed when a stranger said, "Hello."

The courthouse wasn't hard to miss. It towered above the town square with its French-style mansard roof and dormer windows—totally out of place. People stared as we got out of the car and headed up the sloped sidewalk to the entrance. I wasn't sure at first what it was they were looking at, but then I glanced down at my outfit and realized my four-inch inseam chino shorts with my camel-brown leather flip-flops and matching day bag probably gave us away as outsiders. I wanted to yell, "Don't you know who my great-great grandpa is?!" Instead, I nodded to a man who exited the courthouse and he nodded back; only after he paused for a moment to light a cigarette. Besides friendly gestures with odd stares, the one thing that most people in the town seemed to have in common was smoking. Everyone had a cigarette, and when I wondered how fog could happen on an otherwise sunny day I realized half of it was likely a haze of carcinogens in the air.

In the courthouse, Dad pointed down a long, narrow hall to a sign that read: *Recorder of Deeds*. The inside of the office was small. One wall was lined with leather-bound books, and the other three walls were pasted with old maps and notices about *this* and *that*. A woman with blonde hair, oversized glasses with translucent pink frames, bangs as high as heaven, and a soft southern voice sat behind a counter made of wood paneling.

"May I help you, Gentlemen?"

"We're here to see some records," Dad answered.

She chuckled. "Well, okay, what kind of records are you needing? I've got marriage records, property deeds—I don't have birth or death records."

Dad leaned on the counter, looked from side to side, and whispered. "We're looking for information on my great-grandpa. Now you ain't gonna believe this, but he was a Missouri outlaw."

The big-banged woman listened curiously. Her eyes caught to Dad's; she never once looked away and nodded her head as if she knew the story, but a sudden tilt of her head and a "huh" gave the impression that she hadn't heard this one before.

"Yep. Part of Quantrill's Raiders. Rode with the James' Gang. He's from here. We've found a bunch of stuff on the computer, but there are some missing pieces to the puzzle."

"This is the right place, if he ever got married or bought property in this county."

"The things is . . ."—Dad pfft'ed and got louder in his tone—"he married two women at the same time! Faked his own death in Texas, and then married my great-grandma right here in Dent County. Wild. Devil. Jim."

"He definitely sounds wild." She walked from behind the counter over to the wall with the leather-bound books. "These here are our marriage records from the 1850s to about 1870." She pointed to a door to the right of the counter. "Everything else from then on is back over in this room."

Dad continued to converse with her about Wild Devil Jim and his antics. He kept going back and forth between the 1860s and 1870s, and whether or not he married my great-great grandmother legally. I walked over to the wall with the leather-bound books. I touched them and imagined my family's stories were kept inside. Things we could not learn from the "computer."

I grabbed one book from 1865, the year the Civil War ended. I thumbed to the J's and tried to find a record for James Jamison. The old pages flirted with my senses. The musty smell of history. The feel of the rag paper as it tickled my thumb and forefinger. I flipped each page with careful precaution. With my finger as a guide, I scanned down the list of sir names beginning with J's.

J-A . . . J-A-M . . . J-A-M-I . . . Jamison. Nope.

I put the book back and grabbed 1867 for no reason other than 1866 didn't speak to me in the same way, and because Dad had mentioned before that was the year Wild Devil Jim escaped off to Texas. Maybe there would be a clue. I continued the scanning method with my finger but didn't find *Jamison* there.

"I think it must've been 1880 or '81," I heard Dad say to the big-banged woman.

She pulled out a set of keys and unlocked the door to the room that held the memories of mostly everyone who had gotten married in Dent County since 1870. The room was walled-in with floor to ceiling shelving that had book after book, covering each year from 1870 until the 1990s.

"Everything after 1995 is electronic," she said as she pulled the keys from the lock. "Feel free to dive in. I'll be out here if you need me."

Dad and I thumbed through every book from 1880 to 1889, going directly to the J's each time and found nothing. Dad remembered hearing that Eliza Morning Star was only fourteen years old when she married Wild Devil Jim, and he believed she was born sometime in the early 1870s. The records on her were as odd and as disjointed as her husband's.

Dad slapped 1889 shut. "Joe, we could be here all day looking through these."

I shouted through the door to the big-banged woman. "Ma'am, excuse me, but we might need your help." She met me at the door and I continued. "We can't seem to find the marriage record for my great-great grandparents. We're not totally sure what year they were married. Is there an easier way to search?"

"Unfortunately, not for these records," she said disappointedly. "Now, we do have property records upstairs in the attic. You might find a clue up there. They ain't in no particular order, but if you're willing to spend the day digging . . . then have at it!"

Oh, Jesus, please let Dad say no.

I looked at Dad with the face of a selfish child because I knew if he had said yes I'd be the one doing the digging. As much as I wanted to help him find the marriage records to maybe put to rest, or confirm, rumors that had flown in our family for years about Wild Devil Jim living a double life, and who Eliza Morning Star was, what we looked for could not be found in any of the records in the Dent County Courthouse. Plus, my hair wax had already begun to melt for a second day, and the dust from the attic would have given that glossy glow on my face a little too much of a matte finish for my liking.

Dad had already been told the stories about Eliza Morning Star when he was growing up, passed down from one person to the next. Even the kids at school, who poked fun at him for his suspiciously tanned skin, added to the stories. When I dug into records online several years back I helped to confirm that her dad was born as Asa Eagle in the Cherokee Nation, and that her mother was born in North Carolina and marked as "Negro." I was perplexed by this find, but, indeed, as far as the rumors confirmed, it was true.

What we've come to learn is that, as a child, Asa Eagle's family was moved westward in 1838 because of the *Indian Relocation Act of 1830*, better known as the *Trail of Tears*. And her family, freed people who lived among the Cherokee, were forced westward as well as a part of the same relocation. Many of the Native peoples and freed slaves left the trail before ever making it to their final destination of Tahlequah, Oklahoma.

Dent County, Missouri, was a stop off on the trail and both families fled at that point, changed their names, and became other people. He became Francis and she became Mary. They grew up together, fell in love, and married. Their daughter was given the name Morning Star, but in public she was known as Eliza. Overtime, they had begun to pass as every day citizens of Dent County because their families pretended to be something they were not. In some ways this can be seen as a cop out, but in other ways it's freeing. Just as Eliza Morning Star gave a smile to those who stared as she shopped the streets of Sligo, it was a *fuck you* to the man. And it's not surprising, with all their name changes and hiding their identities alongside those bandits who slipped into the back country to road agent a train, that Eliza Morning Star grew up to marry a rebel outlaw.

Even though I don't carry the desire to ride into a town

and shoot every Yank around, and I've never been in a situation where I had to change my name and become someone else, the misfit blood had always run through my veins. Through *our* veins. Motivations have been different, but Dad and I were people who had always wanted to be free and had fought, in our own ways, every chance we got. People who lived our lives authentically, even if it meant having to run.

Maybe Wild Devil Jim would be proud of his liberal queer great-great grandson after all.

Dad answered the big-banged woman before I could. "Nah, that's all right. We should probably head back on over to Steelville anyway."

I was relieved and okay with holding on to family stories. Dusty files in the attic of an old courthouse wouldn't tell us anything we hadn't already known about who we were anyhow.

WE PULLED out of Salem the same as we had entered. We watched folks in herds of four and five who walked along enjoying the day, their conversations, and their cigarettes. I wanted to talk to Dad about his love for Donald Trump and how I couldn't understand, or see, that a person whose blood beat liberty through his veins could support a man like him. I wanted to talk to Dad about racism. About how our family, if we couldn't have passed for white, would have been taken down by a man like Trump. That someone like me, who could pass as a white boy, hasn't been extended all of the privileges that Dad, who could also pass, has had because of who I was as a gay man in America and who he was as a straight man. I wanted to talk about how someone like Trump could take away my civil rights as a gay man, and possibly the one thing that was more important to me than anything else—my marriage with my husband, Cory.

I told Dad I'd been struck by Wild Devil Jim's and Eliza Morning Star's stories ever since we learned who they really were. That I could see a little bit of both of them in us. "But were they able to cover up who they *really* were that well?"

"Everybody knew, Joe. She moved in with us when she got older, and all the kids would tease me and say, 'Hey, Dave, where's your nigger grandma?'"

Words are powerful and carry pain. They have the ability to give us light or to take it away. Hearing Dad say what the kids called his great-grandmother sent a pain to my heart, and I felt it in my head. Just as if Jacob had slammed me into the slate desktop and called me a faggot.

Dad stared forward, tears in his eyes. "I'd tell them she wasn't that word. She was my great-grandma and she was beautiful and loving."

In high school some of the guys on Dad's basketball team joked and told him he was a great player because of his great-grandmother. Because of her roots. Because of what they thought Black people could and couldn't do. He'd brush it off, and they'd let it go because he was the high scorer on the team. They gave him a pass, but they were quick to remind him of why they thought he could jump so high. But if you saw Dad and me, we're as white as can be. I have gray-green eyes, olive skin, and my now dark hair was blonde when I was a child. My aquiline nose gives away my Native American heritage more than it does my African. Most of the time, I get asked if I'm Italian. And a few times

I've answered *yes* because it was easier to say that than to explain my complex background.

We often act how the world perceives us. So easy to pass for what others want—or expect—*us* to be.

I guess it's always been that way. Like divides that amplify our differences, it's biological. Inherited from our ancestors to look and act and be something we're not. Often it comes easy and other times it doesn't.

Our family story is one example of the cultural fiction America has been so obsessed with over time. If a person presented one way, they were *this*. If a person presented another, they were *that*. Even if they weren't *this* or *that*. There was no room for the in between. No space for difference. Only boxes that one must tick, and whatever box was ticked opened opportunity or misfortune. Race is fiction but racism is not.

The truth was, no matter how dark the skin was of some of our family members, we, as a family, had some privileges because of how we presented ourselves to the world and how the world, in return, accepted us to be.

But if there was one thing Dad couldn't hide, it was his hillbilly ways. A byproduct of his rural upbringing that now existed as part of his aura. He could hide his Blackness and Native heritage and pass as a white guy same as me, but his southern draw, colloquialisms, and do-it-yourself-jimmy-rigging mentality hadn't allowed him to pass as anything other than a hillbilly in Indiana. And the one thing I couldn't hide was my gayness. I could straighten my walk, deepen my voice, and pump iron as much as the next guy, but I was most comfortable accepting the sissy way that I walked, along with my inflections, and my overall queerness. And that stuck out in Indiana as well, for better or for worse.

Hillbilly, queer. Dad, son.

To pass or not to pass? Do we or don't we? Connected or strangers?

I've been embarrassed by my hillbilly roots for a long, long time. Hillbilly, after all, was a term—and in many ways a persona—created by the white elite to wield its power and separate the classes. It was built on a stereotype. But *hillbilly* was the culture I grew up in, and one I didn't begin to recognize as different until I was in high school. My mom, her family, they were hillbillies, too. Many of the kids in Cowan were hillbillies, but the newer kids in Cowan, who lived in the fields that the other kids' families used to plow, were not.

I was a newer kid. One whose family was not old Cowan, but I wasn't like the other *new* kids. I was a hillbilly. It was in the way I talked, the types of jobs Dad and Mom held, and it defined what type of future I might have. It was everything I didn't want, and the only way to not end up like other hillbillies was to pretend not to be one because there's a lot of opportunity out there waiting if that class line can be crossed. If one can learn to whisper the right words at the right time, while carrying their things in the right type of bag sewn by the best designer . . . *you* can pass. "It's okay to come this way," they said.

As I got older, my gayness, in many ways, hid my hillbilly roots, as did my education and anything else I sought as an escape from Cowan or the similarities I had with other hillbillies, like Dad. They said education was the great equalizer, but it's also the great divider. Denying parts of who we are can create acceptance, and it can also tear us apart.

I could begin to understand why Dad was pained when he'd get teased by the kids at school. When one tried hard to be something they weren't, it created a fear and anger deep within that was always at the surface, waiting to pop through the skin to reveal itself. It's a vulnerable place, and it's frightening. I was there for many years before I embraced my gayness and became comfortable in my own skin, and I needed to get to the same place with my hillbilly roots; even if I didn't identify with rural culture anymore.

Understanding my roots, and not ignoring them, would be the only way for me to understand how Dad and I had grown so far apart. And in so many ways, that's what I kept reminding myself that the trip was all about. It wasn't only my gayness and atheism and politics that separated me from Dad. It was a class divide. Just as Dad needed to work to accept his background, to overcome the anger and fear when kids would question how high he jumped or how dark his great-grandmother's skin was, I, too, had to accept what it meant to be a hillbilly son of a hillbilly Dad.

Trump's vision for America had given many people a free ticket to continue to bury truths; to see things at a surface level. Black and white. *Libtards* or *hard-working patriots*. Pointed fingers said, "You don't belong!"

Shedding lies and embracing truths can be both painful and freeing.

Not long after I turned twenty-one, I wanted to have my first gay bar experience. I gathered a couple of friends and we drove to downtown Muncie to explore the only gay establishment in the city. Nervous about what to expect and afraid of being found out, we parked blocks away and ducked into alleys to traverse our way through the shadows.

Before we entered the front doors to a place filled with people like me, an old, beat-up truck with a terrible exhaust system rumbled to a stop in front of the bar. I'll never forget the look in the driver's eyes as he stared at us and yelled, "Faggots!" It was a look of disgust and anger. Two years prior, Matthew Shepard, another college student about my age, was beaten in Laramie, Wyoming, and tied to a fence. He died six days later; all because he was gay and wouldn't hide who he was. Those were the first moments in my life I realized being me could actually get me killed, and "faggot" always took me back to Jacob.

Just after freshman year of college, Steve and I broke up. I was home for the summer, and Jacob called. He'd heard about my coming out and said he wanted to talk. My inner-voice told me not to go, but I was desperate and alone. All of my college friends were in their hometowns for the summer, and my group of friends from high school had gone their separate ways—some married, some out of state, others too busy on that particular evening.

Jacob picked me up in his old beat-up Dodge truck. He honked the horn three times to let me know he had arrived. Before getting in, I poked my head through the rolled down passenger window and rested my arms on the door.

"Hey," I said.

"Hey," he said.

We stared at one another for a moment, trying to find our old selves through years of change. I wondered if I should actually get in, and in my mind questioned Jacob's motives. *Does he really just want to talk? Will I be safe?*

He had been a jerk to me for years, but beyond his shaggy mousy-brown hair and five-o-clock shadow I saw a forlorn expression on his face that reminded me of those days when we played dolls and built forts.

"Your hair—it's different," he said. "I like it."

I had cut my shoulder-length hair from high school days into a Caesar and bleached it platinum blonde. I smiled and shrugged my shoulders. "Thanks!"

I hopped in.

We headed out onto the desolate country roads, nothing else around other than shoulder-high fields of corn that watched over our cruise. He slowed to a stop near a grove of trees that hung ominously across the road; their shadows created the only darkness on that late-July evening. I thought for a moment that I had made a mistake and that would be where it all ended for me. Jacob would kill me there and get off by claiming the *gay panic defense* and he would ask those at his church to forgive him. He wouldn't even have to dump the body. He reached into his pocket and pulled out a pouch. *A knife?* I wondered.

Jacob pointed to the glovebox and asked me to grab the manual. I handed it to him and he unfolded the pouch and dumped brownish-green finely chopped contents onto it. "Wanna get high?" he said.

We smoked and coughed and then sat in silence for a few moments. He took a deep breath, coughed again, and spurt out some words in between. He asked me about college—if it were true that I'd come out. I told him it was. My mind drifted back to all of those junior high and high school days. The gay-slurs, his pleas for forgiveness. I began to question why I'd put myself in the same situation, after a year of building myself up and coming to terms with who I was.

Jacob cocked his head back and to the side and turned his glazed-over eyes my way. He moved the manual from his lap and threw it on the dashboard. Sprinkles of pot rained to the floor. He placed his hand on mine and gently rubbed his thumb across the top before letting go. He patted the middle of the bench seat, flashed a crooked smile, and signaled for me to skootch on over. Trying to find a connection back to whatever we once had, I did.

He slapped my thigh and squeezed. He kept his eyes locked on mine as I heard the teeth of his zipper scream open. I didn't look. He motioned downward with his head. "You wanna suck it?" The memory of the pain in my face from the slate top table pounded through my mind. My fist clinched. I closed my eyes and wished for time travel, to be taken back to only a few hours before to a denial of his invitation.

I opened my eyes wide. The cab of the truck narrowed in. I lost my breath and gasped for air. Through the haze I managed to shake my head back and forth.

No! I wanted to scream.

Instead, the sounds of cicadas and crickets rose up from the fields. He moved his hand to my head and massaged it with his fingertips for a moment before he lowered me down into his abyss, his silver and red confederate flag belt buckle with two musket guns across the top caught the light and blinded my way. His hand guided my head throughout the journey. I gave him what he wanted.

After I was done, he zipped up, started the truck, and drove back to my parents' house. No words were spoken;

though I continued to wonder during the drive if I would die.

I got out of the cab without saying goodbye. The door was barely closed when he threw the truck into reverse and squealed his tires as he pulled away.

Jacob hadn't forced me to do anything. I went, and performed, at my own submission. But had I done it only because I feared what the outcome would be if I hadn't?

I cried all night, staring at the popcorn ceiling above my bed, confused by what I had done; what fuel I had thrown on the fire. I had fully revealed my true self in so many ways. *Would it cost me my life? Could I pull the covers up and make it all disappear?*

We never spoke again, and that felt okay—and *safe*—for me. Years later, I heard that he got heavy into drugs and found himself in rehab, where he met his future wife. I wondered if he ever prayed for forgiveness, for falling victim to the needle, or for being led astray by that queer he once called his friend. Did he run across the yard, hoping for someone to watch his back from the evil force that lurked beyond?

6

AFTER SALEM, Dad told me he wanted to stop off to see his old girlfriend, Lila. She worked in a little diner in Steelville, and he hadn't seen in her in a while but they'd kept up with each other over the years. "Now, don't go telling your mom. You won't believe this, but she's been married four times!"

I was curious to see Lila. I'd never met any of Dad's old girlfriends, and I was dying for a bite to eat. I wondered if she was cute. Maybe short and petite like Mom. She led Dad to Christ, so I wouldn't have been surprised if she wore a prayer covering and donned a cross. But considering she'd been married four times, she probably wore some seriously saucy lingerie.

Dad swung open the door to the diner, letting off clangs and jingles from the bells tied to the top. An elderly woman with short gray hair, glasses, and wrinkled skin wiped down a table in the corner. I looked past her and around to see if anyone else worked the diner. Anyone who might fit the description of Lila I'd built in my mind.

The woman looked up from the table. "David!"

"Lila Sears!"

She tossed the sopping rag onto the table and walked our way. Her pursed lips tried to hide her smile. "It's Lila Johnson now."

Well, not what I expected. She seemed way older than Dad, and not quite as trampy as I had dreamed up. But they did meet at church and were baptized together, so maybe she was a good Christian girl. It had been five years since they'd seen each other last. When Dad broke it off with her all those years ago, calling from the payphone outside of Shreveport, they never really hung up for good. Every time he rolled into Steelville, he stopped by the diner to see her. It had become platonic, and yet she was something he couldn't let go of. She was a constant connection to his past life. A reminder of what he once was—the one who sunk baskets into hoops as the students of Steelville High jumped from their seats and erupted in applause.

Dad and Lila bantered with each other. Dad threw out off-colored statements and Lila responded with witty remarks to see who could make the other laugh first.

Dad lost.

Lila was good. She kept her smile pursed and wouldn't relent until Dad laughed and then she'd let go.

It was a romance that had sparked long before I was ever thought of, and I felt like an interloper. Awkwardly watching these two was like stepping back in time to see what life would have been like had my dad married his high school sweetheart. Like Marty McFly in *Back to the Future*, I felt myself slowly fading away. It was the two of them, alone, connected.

Even though they had moved on, Dad twice and Lila, well, four times, there was still a spark in their eyes. When Dad told me that he and Lila had stayed in touch I was surprised. It felt like that was a betrayal to Mom. But seeing the two of them together reminded me that love doesn't always die. Even when lovers go their separate ways and end up marrying other people and building lives with them, past experiences are there forever and feelings don't always stop.

After Dad found the letter from Steve on the kitchen table, our love was out in the open. At least with Dad. Steve and I were a permanent fixture for the next year, and then we broke it off because he left Ball State without intentions of coming back. His hometown was four hours away. In the life of a nineteen-year-old, that distance might as well have been 14 hours—and a few thousand miles—away. That was before the widespread use of cellphones and Facebook—and most forms of social media wouldn't be invented for another seven years. Our only connection outside of landlines and snail mail was dial-up AOL. Why would we have tried to make it work?

Steve and I experienced many firsts together in that year. Months before Jacob took me on that summer drive in his truck, Steve rented a room at a Holiday Inn on the outskirts of Muncie. He scrounged up what change he had to pay for the night, and he lined the edges of the chest-of-drawers in the room with off-white votive candles. Third Eye Blind sang *Motorcycle Drive By* in the background, as we both fumbled our fingers and legs here and there trying to figure it all out under the dim candlelight. It was my first time, and his first time sleeping with another guy. We both fell truly, madly in love. It was the figuring it all out that brought us together. The learning how to date and how be in love without letting too many people know for fear of how they'd respond. Even though Steve told me to cross that line at college orientation, it was best to hide who were to the outside world in 1997. Like Third Eye Blind sang on that song, never so alone and never so alive.

Steve was an excellent writer and he wrote me love notes every day. He passed them to me when we met in his dorm room after class. I held them out in front of me and read each line as I pursed my lips and tried to hide a smile. He went in for a tackle and encased me with his solid football arms as we both landed on his bed in laughter. We held each other in the safety of the room because we couldn't be like that outside of those walls.

I was safe there. *We* were safe.

One day after class I met him in his room, but instead of a tackle onto the bed he stood with a letter in his hand; a wide smile on his face. His eyes illuminated with anticipation as he read each line, over and over. What he held was not for me. Steve told me he was leaving.

I was heartbroken. My eyes didn't hold the same anticipation. My eyes were blurred out from the tears. I couldn't see—I *didn't* want to see—and I tried to find the words but as soon as they made it to the tip of my tongue, my lips pursed too hard and they wouldn't come out. I didn't understand, but he tried to explain that his brother had gotten him on at a factory in their town and he'd make beaucoup bucks. He shook the letter at me. "Why waste my time here when I can start life now?"

Start life now. Without me.

The painful truth is that we don't always get to stay with

the ones we love. Those we experienced so many firsts with. At that moment in my life, I could have locked the door and spent an eternity in that dorm room with Steve. No one else on the outside mattered to me. If he wouldn't have broken it off for that opportunity back home in the factory, then I probably never would have tried to experience life beyond him.

Like Third Eye Blind continued to sing—as Steve and I connected our bodies as one, and made promises that never made it beyond that Holiday Inn or Room 922 of Palmer Hall—I knew I could never have you.

It's interesting to think about the *what-could-have-beens*. But those thoughts, had they materialized, wouldn't have led me to my husband Cory, or possibly not even on the trip with Dad. Instead, I enjoyed the next sixteen years being Steve's friend and watched his life blossom from afar—the same way Dad and Lila stayed in each other's lives. I spent our *friendship years* learning from Steve. Our relationship, beyond love, helped shape the person I am today. And Steve would have argued I did the same for him. We supported each other through long-distance exchanges, even when others in our lives had no idea we had kept open our line of communication.

When Steve left Ball State, we continued our letter writing, but instead of passing them to each other in person, we reverted back to snail mail. Over time, snail mail turned into email and then into texting. We each built our own lives but as we did, we were there for one another, from afar, to challenge and support the decisions we made.

When I started dating a guy named Andrew about a year after we broke it off, Steve was the first to tell me that

Andrew wasn't right for me. And even though he'd never met Andrew, he was correct. It took me walking in on him with his legs wrapped around a fifty-year-old man he'd met on the Internet to prove that Steve was right.

When I went to graduate school to study Higher Education Administration, Steve, who saw the writing on the wall as factories packed up and left town, re-enrolled as an undergraduate at a regional campus near his hometown. I helped him, through our emails, re-navigate the system of higher education.

When Cory and I started dating, Steve began a romance with a heart surgeon twice our age. While he gave my relationship with Cory a blessing, I was critical of his and he eventually broke it off.

The day he graduated from college, I sent him a text and told him how proud I was of him. I did the same when he decided not to pursue a job in his field of study but went to pilot's school instead and became a commercial pilot.

When Cory and I got married, he texted me and told me I was a lucky guy. Though he wished he could've been there to congratulate us, encasing me in his solid arms, he jokingly said it was hard to see me go off the market.

On rare occasions, Steve would have to pick up an extra leg to Indianapolis during his daily commercial flight route from Cleveland to Chicago to Kansas City and back again. Whenever that happened, he texted me, and we reunited in person at the airport for a few hours. But like Dad and Lila, our face-to-face meetings only happened a handful of times over the years. The last time Steve and I met, he told me he had fallen for someone and they were engaged to be married. "He's the one," he said. "Who I'll spend the rest of my life with."

I was so happy for him. We embraced, looked at each other with pursed lips that broke into smiles, and then we each lost our old game and fell into laughter. We were far from hiding behind dorm room walls, but also no need to care. We had both come to publicly accept who we were.

When we let go, Steve turned, headed toward his gate, and walked out of my life for the last time. His final text to me was about an old fixer-upper Piper plane that he and his fiancé had purchased. I later learned that it had some mechanical issues. Steve chose to fly it from the airport where he kept it to another one sixty miles away for mainte-nance. The plane never made it more than one hundred feet off the ground before it crashed down on a prairie road outside of the airport's property. Steve died instantly.

When Steve died, I didn't learn about his death for three weeks. No one knew they should let me know, even though we had existed as integral components of each other's lives for more than fifteen years. I learned of his death from a post on Facebook that his sister put on his page. We had no mutual friends. Still, to this day, I have no idea how his sister's post ended up in my newsfeed. If something happened to Dad or to Lila, I imagined the same would be true for them. No one in their lives would think to let either of them know.

I watched Dad with Lila and saw many comparisons to my relationship with Steve. A love that never died but instead turned into a friendship, a support system, albeit secretive and from afar. Perhaps that's the only way for rela-tionships we don't want to die to continue to live; the rela-tionships that shape us into who we are, even when the person isn't with us physically day to day. But knowing they are out there, existing, guides our daily paths and decisions. Steve gave me the confidence to be who I was, in all of the moments that followed, in the months and years after Dad read the letter that outed me. And Lila brought Dad closer to God, and that experience gave him the confidence to believe that everything in this world could be forgiven even when others, including his own son, believed otherwise.

Dad grabbed Lila's hand and took a look at her diamond-studded wedding band. He squeezed her fingers, then let them slip away one by one. They looked at each other with a farewell smile.

"If I don't make it this way again, I'll see you in Heaven." Dad said.

"It'll be one hell of a party!" Lila said and gave Dad a wink.

We pulled away from the parking lot and headed toward the main road. Dad never mentioned Lila again. Even though Steve was on the tip of my tongue, and I had so many questions I wanted to ask Dad about the day he found the letter, my lips stayed pursed and I kept silent.

———

TRAVERSING the winding highways of central Missouri was our time to get lost and found, to uncover our uncomfortable truths. Trapped together. No one but us. We passed a boarded up house that the last tenants walked away from without ever allowing anyone else to call it home. I admired its immaculately carved Victorian gingerbread trim that was juxtaposed to its peeling light pink paint. It was plopped out of somewhere in time and placed along the highway next to some plastic bags from Piggly Wiggly that blew in the wind.

Dad started to laugh and tried to say something, but his words wouldn't get past his wheezing. He beat the steering wheel with the palms of his hands.

"Are you making fun of me?" I said.

Dad shook his head no and finally got the words out in short spurts. He told me he once got married in that house.

"What? To who?"

A few weeks before he blew up the quad in Bible college, Dad had devised a plan with this wild girl from New Jersey—who was only there to earn her M.R.S. and who really wanted him to be the one to give her that degree. But he was with Lila and this girl really wasn't his type. But she was his match, in humor at least.

Dad guffawed and slapped the steering wheel harder. "But her face resembled a Bull Terrier wearing a Brenda Lee wig."

None of the guys wanted her, and three months into the academic year she had given up hope that she would ever walk down the aisle. But Dad thought of a way to make her happy while having a little fun.

"One weekend we got this idea to wake up the nearest Justice of the Peace. Tell him she was pregnant, and that we had to get married right away. So he married us in the living room of that house."

Tears of this joyful memory now gathered in the corners of Dad's eyes.

Half sleepy-eyed, the Justice of the Peace asked for their marriage license and the fee. His wife, still in her kerchief, had a pen out ready to sign as a witness. Dad, and Bull-Terrier-Brenda-Lee, told them they didn't have a license or any money. The Justice of the Peace didn't live up to his title and cussed them up and down and out the front door. His wife followed behind with a wooden roller in her hand. Dad and his "bride" jumped into his car and sped away, screaming and laughing, popping open a beer he'd swiped from his dad's stash.

I chuckled at the story. I did. I mean, it was funny as hell. But there was irony in it, and the irony was what hurt. Especially when Cory and I tried so many times to get married, and more than once that right was taken away from us.

We tried in 2005, as outlaws ourselves, first married during a commitment ceremony because our marriage wasn't recognized by the State of Indiana or the federal government. Our next wedding came in 2014 when a federal judge struck down the marriage ban in Indiana, but our marriage was then terminated by the State the same day. We found out about it from a CNN Breaking News push notification on our phones. On October 6th of that same year, our marriage was reinstated when the 7th Circuit Court of Appeals ruled that Indiana must recognize all same-sex marriages. And then, of course, marriage equality came to every state in the summer of 2015.

The day Cory and I were legally married we rushed to the Delaware County Courthouse in Muncie, Indiana, to get our license. We had only a matter of hours before a stay went into place like it had in every other state where the ban on same-sex marriage had fallen. So our window of opportunity was short.

We were the first in line when the courthouse opened at 8:00 a.m. Four women sat at the counter in the Clerk's office, and beyond them several others sat at desks. No one looked up to make eye contact with us; no one asked if we needed help.

After standing in line for what seemed like an eternity, I finally spoke up. "Hello? We're here to get our marriage license."

Cory grabbed at the back of my shirt, his way to let me know I was being what he called, *J.R. bitchy*, and that I needed to slow my roll.

One woman at the counter looked up. She made eye contact with me, over to Cory, and then back to me. With no expression on her face, she got up and walked toward the sea of desks behind her and bent down to talk closely to another woman seated at a desk in the last row. The woman at the desk looked up as the woman from the counter pointed in our direction. Both walked toward us.

The woman from the counter took her seat. She shuffled papers and looked in every other direction of that room except for ours. The woman from the desk walked us through all of the proper documents, showed us where to sign, folded everything up and into an envelope, and said congratulations. She handed our legal future to us across the countertop.

That's it? All of the fighting and laws and court hearings over that?

It seemed so simple and so harmless. Pieces of paper in an envelope that did nothing more than make a fourteen-year relationship legal. No longer would we need to worry about things such as hospital visitation, our finances, taxes, or even what would happen if one of us unexpectedly died. Beyond being husbands, we had become each other's next of kin; not in ceremony, but by law. Even though the act of handing it all over to us in an envelope seemed so simple, it was a day I never thought I'd see. At least not in Indiana.

We left the courthouse in another rush. Even though we had the papers, we had to get them signed by a minister, witnesses, and return them to the courthouse to be filed. Without those last steps, the papers in the envelope meant nothing.

At 9:00 a.m. that morning Cory and I were married at the base of Beneficence, an angel statue on the campus of Ball State University that stands for freedom and perseverance. In one hand "Benny" holds a treasure chest, while her other hand is open, arm outstretched, to give the gift of knowledge, wisdom, and charity to those who grace her presence. It was the perfect place to start our new, legal life.

We held hands as our own Justice of the Peace told a small gathering of friends and family about the night Cory and I met. He had come uninvited to a house party my roommates had thrown, and tripped over our grill—bouncing hot coals across the yard where people ran in every direction to dump their libations onto the flames—and he stumbled my way to tell me *I* was the hottest thing he'd ever seen. Our small gathering laughed as the Justice of the Peace transitioned into a story about how when two containers of sand are poured together, they become one—indistinguishable from when they were in their own spaces.

Dad and Mom were there that day, and Dad told me how proud he was that we'd taken the leap. "Fuck them, Joe. Fuck all those assholes who say you shouldn't get married."

Well, that was his way of saying it.

As the first same-sex couple to marry in Delaware County that morning, the feeling was one I'd never felt. Sure, we'd been "married" nine years before in a commitment ceremony, but this time it was different. It was as if the moment we sealed our vows with a kiss the world changed. The sun shone brighter, birds sung louder, and I had an enormous weight lifted from my shoulders. That all lasted until seven hours later when a judge issued a stay and our marriage was put on hold for the next four months.

We were legally married but no one would legally recognize it. For the days and weeks after, my only encouragement was a statement issued by the State of Indiana that existed at the top of our signed marriage license: "What therefore God hath joined together, let no man put asunder." Although I didn't believe in God, Mike Pence, the Governor of Indiana, did—and this encouragement felt like I had taken Dad's advice and said, "Fuck all you assholes."

So marriage to us was no joke. And as much as I wanted to continue to laugh about Dad's escapade with Bull-Terrier-Brenda-Lee and the sleepy Justice of the Peace, and them pretending to not know they had to have the proper paperwork, I couldn't stop thinking of the day Cory and I got our papers that we fought so hard for. And on that day, we saw all the couples on the news who stood on steps of courthouses in small Indiana towns, finally taking the plunge into lives they'd always dreamed of. And I remembered how Dad wrapped his arms around the two of us at the same time, kissed both of our heads, and told us how proud he was.

When something I wanted so badly had been toyed with

by elected politicians and ignorant folks, sometimes the slightest of things pissed me off. Even if it hadn't directly impacted me. And even if it were funny, like Dad's fake marriage.

I giggled to lighten my tone. "I'm just thinking about how Cory and I couldn't get married for so long . . . so we had to do it without proper paperwork the first time. Were we considered married . . . like, in your eyes?"

Dad stopped smiling. I don't think my fake giggle had lightened the tone. I had either pissed *him* off or made him think. Perhaps one in the same. I thought about what to say next, anything, but nothing came. And then Dad beat me to it. "Well, it was different times. We were kids . . . just goofing off and having fun." He stared straight on at the highway.

I knew I had fucked up. It was a funny story. I laughed. I wanted to laugh again to let him know I agreed that it was different times, but I wanted to argue. I wanted to show him that these little privileges in life, like marriage and skin color, and who is allowed to do what and when, and who makes those rules and why . . . *How was any of it fair?* How had twenty years of not talking about who we were, and what I'd become, allowed him to think these stories of a time gone by were okay? That casting his vote for a man like Trump wasn't a fuck you to the man, but a fuck you to me?

Somehow, I didn't have it in me. I mean, I had all of the thoughts in my head. All of the things I wanted to say, but the words wouldn't come. Since the previous day, each time I wanted to push Dad, a little, so we could have conversations that bridged our differences, I gave up shy of crossing the line that divided us. The line I, perhaps, also helped to create.

But really the hesitation was biological. It had always been there. The divide. Our stark differences are what I liked, what I *loved* actually, about us. Our dad and son relationship. Our friendship. But sometimes it held me back from saying what I would say to any other person I disagreed with. I wanted Dad to speak for his party, the party of Donald Trump, and I wanted him to apologize for everything they stood for; all of the times they tried to deny me my marriage. I wanted to argue with him to argue with "the party."

Were his words, when I got married, in vain? Why couldn't he understand what it was like to be me? He'd been there for me through coming out, my attempts at getting married, and always telling me to be me. In that moment I wanted him to speak so I could've had the courage to formulate the words to argue. But the truth was, words were shallow. Actions were deep.

So when it comes to family divides, building a bridge is what works. Meeting each other in the middle. *Right?* If we went off the bridge and scaled down that rocky wall into those deep cracks, it's a dark place. That's why there's the saying, "Don't talk politics or religion with family." Because between Dad and me, below our bridge, much of our differences seemed to be political. Connected to the election and Dad's support for Donald Trump. But honestly, I'd come to realize that it was much deeper. It was class. It was religion. It was sexuality. All of those can be political, but they're real issues affecting everyday lives. *Our* lives. Everything that always seemed like a difference we could span was now magnified and heated, and everything at the bottom in those deep dark cracks had begun to boil to the top.

I thought of Rick and Leslie's son, Silas, and my parting words that I spoke only to him within my mind: *I hope you find your way out of here to a better life, but don't leave your dad behind.*

Instead of pushing the conversation, I chose to be a coward. I stayed on the bridge and looked away. I didn't want to face what had made its way up from the deep dark cracks below. Instead, we drove on to the Sligo Cemetery.

THE CHAIN-LINK FENCE around the final resting place of Wild Devil Jim and Eliza Morning Star was as rusted as the brownish-red earth that held the bones of all of those who had come and gone through Sligo over the last two centuries. Other than the former residents who were permanently a part of the town, not much was left other than the fallen-in remains of a few homes, and an overgrown railroad track that led off into a pasture of waist-high golden grass. A reminder that the town was once a place called home by those who rest in the Sligo Cemetery. A place where Eliza Morning Star walked down Main Street in search of those new inventions to make life as a wife and mother a little easier. A place where townsfolk gawked as she nodded.

Inside the fence of the cemetery was a different story. Someone had taken the time to keep up with everything. Weeds around headstones were non-existent; the gravel drive that circled the outer edges was freshly laid; and bushes next to benches were trimmed.

Dad put his hand up to his forehead and wiped sweat from his brow. "Phew, it's a hot son-of-a-bitch out here today, ain't it?" I agreed with a nod.

We left the gravel drive and cut through the middle of the cemetery. I examined each headstone we passed, and made estimations on how long it had been since a loved one had visited. The lack of any kind of flowers on the graves led me to believe that it had been some time.

The saddest of all were the babies. The stones that indicated only one year for both birth and death. Some of the stones were alone, as if the family had moved on to another life and had been buried elsewhere. And others were right next to their parents, even though the parents had lived on another sixty years and likely had other kids who grew up to have kids, and lives, far from this forgotten town. Then there were several graves of children, all of whom had died between the mid-1940s and early 1950s. Polio, probably, or maybe TB.

When had this town become extinct? When had people stopped burying their dead here? When had they last visited these graves, put down a flower, and walked away knowing they'd never be back?

I realized I was there, so many years after their deaths, walking by, thinking about their lives, and headed toward the graves of my great-great grandparents who I never knew in their lifetime. Only beyond their deaths. I hadn't brought anything to leave behind, to show those who may come after us, even if only the caretaker, that someone else had been there to remember the dead.

"Right there"—Dad pointed toward two modest headstones—"that's them."

Next to each other but not together. Other than *Jamison* as their last name, there was no indicator to link the two as married. Because of the distance in their births and deaths, they could have been father and daughter. They could have been cousins. They could have been any relation other than husband and wife. Their graves sat a good four feet apart.

Dad gestured toward a shaded slope that was the last part of the cemetery before the fence divided it from a heavily wooded area. "Granny used to be down over that way. She was buried by herself until someone moved her up here, 'bout ten years ago."

Eliza Morning Star died in her sleep at ninety years old. Being buried down the hill in a shaded area, far from Wild Devil Jim, said more than she had in her lifetime about those secrets she kept. Dad said he thought maybe it was her wishes to be buried alone; that she hadn't wanted to be buried near an outlaw. Perhaps she never forgave Wild Devil Jim for his crimes, or taking her from her family. But maybe she did really love him. We'd never know for sure. Even though she encouraged dad to be brave until her final days, after Wild Devil Jim had gone the world around her hadn't allowed the right words that could've shown Dad what being brave really meant. But the nuance of it all existed. Wild Devil Jim had allowed her to go where she wanted when she wanted. Was it at the cost of being forced to run from who she was?

I asked Dad who moved her after all that time. He said one of his cousins, who lived down in New Orleans, decided she needed to be up the hill next to her husband. They sent the money to have it done, and, eighty-one years after they had last laid side by side, some undertaker from over in Salem placed Eliza Morning Star next to Wild Devil Jim.

I wondered if they hadn't been buried together because she had been mixed, even though they lived their lives otherwise. But in death, it was harder to control the narrative. Dad had said everyone knew the rumors were true, and I wondered if in 1960 rural Missouri the truth was too much for this small town.

The sloped, shaded area where Eliza Morning Star had once been buried didn't hold any other graves. She had been there, by herself, for over forty years before she was reunited with her husband seven yards up the hill in a sunnier area. I positioned myself at the base of the four-foot space that separated them. A space between two people who lived their lives as they wanted without any terms and conditions from others. Though I wondered what terms and conditions had been placed on her, by Wild Devil Jim, to hide who she really was.

Maybe the two of them had tried their best to show toughness and bravery, by their own definitions. Maybe they had loved each other, and that love never died.

7

My phone rang out a xylophone version of the *American Beauty* theme song and broke up the dead air in the old Sligo Cemetery. It hadn't rung all day. I told Dad I needed to walk away for a minute. Cory called, and at the perfect time. I needed an escape back to my world. But I knew the news was likely not good.

The morning I left for Missouri I awoke to the smell of vomit heavy throughout the house. One puddle to the next led from the hallway into the living room, onto the rug, and then up our faux leather coach. When you wake up to puddles of puke throughout your house, you know someone had a bad night or a really good night. But when you're thirty-seven and live with your husband and two dogs, it's not likely the puke came from humans and a wild night of partying.

I slammed the bedroom door and had hoped it would startle Cory awake. I screamed out at our eleven-year-old English Setter, Sally, and told her she was a little bitch. It was a term I used mostly for endearment, but also one I used when I meant business. No wonder why Sally always seemed so confused.

I knew the puke throughout the house wasn't her fault, but it felt better all the same to point the finger at something. She had not kept her food down for the previous two days and I was tired of cleaning it up. It wasn't uncommon for her to puke every now and then—she always had a sensitive stomach and had been on a special oatmeal-based food for the past eight years—but the amount of puke that now adorned our mid-century modern was extreme.

A whimper from the other room stopped me in my tracks and brought me back to reality. Sally *was* sick. She lay on the dining room floor under the table. I moved one chair out of the way, kneeled to the ground, poked my head under, leaned in, and kissed her. She didn't even look up at me. Her eyes, glazed over, rolled into the back of her head. I wasn't so sure she'd be all right. Those past two days were different than all the other times she had thrown up because of her sensitive stomach.

We adopted Sally when she was five months old. We got her from a pheasant hunter who auctioned dogs at the Country Club, and every dog was sold but Sally. After the auction, we asked him what would happen with her, and he told us he planned to shoot her since no one wanted her. She was the runt of the litter and wouldn't make a good hunting dog. He still made us pay two-hundred dollars for her. He said her retail value was twelve-hundred and we could take her or leave her. We weren't about to let him kill the poor thing, so we paid the two-hundred and she became ours.

From the moment we brought Sally into our house I knew she was special. Not only in the loving sense, but she was a dainty dog with severe anxiety issues. I guess I would've been, too, had I been weaned from my mom by an angry, old pheasant hunter who always threatened to shoot me.

At the time we had another dog, Shafer, a Brittany Spaniel mix. Shafer did not like Sally. When the introduction between the two dogs happened, Shafer went right for Sally and Sally leapt into my arms. I cradled her like a baby and she looked up at me with her pinkish-brown eyes and in that moment, when my eyes met hers, she became my girl. The safety of my arms is what kept her from Shafer for the several years that followed; even after Sally outgrew Shafer and she became too big for me to hold. Sally's habit of jumping into my arms transitioned into a nightly ritual of jumping into my lap, curling up, and falling asleep as my arms embraced her head against my chest.

Sally and Shafer were our kids. Because Cory and I don't have children, we spoiled our dogs. We talked to them in baby voices: "Who's daddy's big girl? Sally's daddy's big girl! Yes you are, you little bitch." We sang children's songs to them. We may have bought a few Ralph Lauren sweaters for them. You know the kind with the Fair Isle print? Don't judge.

I walked down the hill to the shaded area where Eliza Morning Star had been buried. Although Cory's call was a break I needed, I stared at his name on my screen and didn't answer. He wanted me to be in the moment with Dad on the trip, and he made me vow not to call him each time something crazy happened. So I resorted to texting. Each time Dad had said or done something that made me feel silenced or contemplative or ready to run, I texted Cory for a connection back to my turf. The place where everything I had created in my new life still stood without a crack. He would text back and remind me that I needed to stay.

So his name on my screen, and the xylophone that rung out through the cemetery, delivered a message that I knew would send me back. And maybe I was done running. But I didn't answer. I let the call go to my voice mail as I stood for a moment where Eliza Morning Star had been buried. A place where the truth had always been below the surface, waiting to pop its way through to reveal the uncomfortableness of not knowing what was next.

I breathed in my surroundings and prepared myself to take on the inevitable. Cory's message was broken up. He seemed urgent and sad. I couldn't tell if it was the bad connection that made his voice quiver or if he had been crying. Nevertheless, I understood the words that said: "We need to make some decisions. Call me."

I went to my missed calls list and scrolled down to Cory's name and tapped it with my thumb. There was a long, silent pause. No connection. I tried again. No luck.

I walked back up the hill toward Dad who still stood at the foot of Wild Devil Jim's and Eliza Morning Star's graves. I told him I couldn't get a connection, and I needed to walk up closer to the road to see if I could get one there.

I walked past all of the graves I had examined before, but this time I didn't stop to pay my respects. I continued to tap my thumb on Cory's name and tried to connect to the world of the living.

Near the front gate that led to the road I finally heard a

ring. I stopped in my tracks and knew I may have found the one area in the cemetery that wasn't a dead spot.

Cory answered in a somber tone.

"Is everything okay?" I asked.

"I've been trying to reach you all morning."

And I hadn't answered. After all of my searching, I hadn't wanted to find the truth that time.

He told me the vet had done a scan that showed a large mass in Sally's chest. It was likely cancerous. She was too weak to undergo surgery to remove it, and she probably wouldn't survive. I began to shake and held back the tears. "So what are our options?"

"The only option is to put her down," he said. "It's going to happen today at 5."

"Can't we push it back, so I can make it home to say goodbye?"

He explained that she wouldn't make it by the time I returned. That I was too far away from home. She was suffering.

The tears came steadily. I shook from head to toe, and I couldn't distinguish if it was from anger or sadness. "I just want to come home."

"You can't. The best thing you can do is finish out the trip with your dad. I'll say goodbye for you."

I took a deep breath and asked him to promise to let me know when it happened. And then we hung up. Even though our call had ended, I stood in the same spot, the only space that allowed a connection to the outside world, for a good five minutes trying to regain my composure. I went from shaking and tears to calmness and deep breaths. I didn't want Dad to see me crying. He'd always been a tough guy. Ever since the locker room incident in high school when Jacob threw the spray deodorant canister at my head, I've heard Dad's voice on constant loop telling me to be tough: *Punch that son-of-a-bitch right in the mouth!* Or at times like these: *Punch life right in the mother-fucking mouth!*

I always thought being brave meant to not cry; to show no pain. And I had done it so well. I hadn't shown bravery with my fists like Dad had encouraged, but I'd done it by learning not to cry when I hurt. When "faggot" was thrown my way.

These lessons I learned from Dad, but I perfected them on stage at Cowan where I stared into a sea of faces shadowed by the dimmed house lights. I knew Mom and Dad were out there, somewhere, but I couldn't make out one silhouette from the next. A spotlight shone into my eyes, but I'd been trained during months of rehearsal not to squint; not to let the stinging pain from the brightness show.

As a 7th grader, I was cast as the lead in *Shotgun Wedding* on the big high school stage. My character, Jeb, was a stereotyped Ozark Mountain hillbilly who was supposed to perform his daughter's wedding as the town's Justice of the Peace, but instead kept sneaking away to sleep off the drink.

To prepare for the part, I watched Dad's every move. Since he was from Missouri, the heart of the Ozarks, my drama teacher suggested I mimic him. I studied him day after day—the way he walked with a strut; his long arms dangled at his side; his deep southern accent pronounced words like Missouri as Miz-ur-ah and Hawai'i as Huh-why-yuh. Each time I stood at the edge of the stage and tried to let out a southern drawl, it'd end with a high-pitched twang that sounded more like the Lady Chablis than Matthew McConaughey. I paused between the squeaks of my voice, and in that silence my drama teacher and cast mates encouraged me to go on. The stage was the one place I felt safe. Where I could be someone else. A place where I felt like I actually belonged. No one threw anything at my head, told me to suck their dick, or slammed me face first into a table. The stage was my platform for confidence.

I took a deep breath and did my lines over and over, an occasional Lady Chablis here and a Matthew McConaughey there. By the time opening night rolled around, I'd perfected a voice that was not my dad's but was a creation all my own. The spotlight burned through my eyes but I never flinched, never teared up from the strain, and I delivered my *y'alls* and *ain'ts* with a booming voice that echoed out into the gymnasium.

After the curtains closed and the house lights were raised, the cast spilled into the audience to meet our parents. Parting through crowds of fathers handing their daughters flowers, I spotted Dad and Mom who beamed with smiles that reached eye to eye. Dad wrapped his arms around me and squeezed tight before pulling back and giving me a noogie on my head. I squealed and laughed in embarrassment and pulled away from his grip the way boys do with their dads when they're coming of age and trying to figure out the space that separates kid from young adult. He leaned down and put his hands on my shoulders. "I'm proud of you. You were so brave."

I WANTED TO BE ALONE, and in the grand scheme of things I was. I was surrounded by five-hundred dead people in a town where no one had lived for nearly forty years. But there was Dad, and my great-great grandparents, and stories about basketball records and track records, and the reunion, and political differences, and many more miles we still had to cover before I could truly be alone.

I wiped the last remaining tear from my right cheek and turned to head back to Dad. As I walked past all of the graves for the third time, I started to think about how short life is. How we are only here for a moment in time and then we're gone. Kind of like Steve. And now, Sally.

If we're lucky enough to have someone who loves us, they'll visit our graves and we'll get flowers and other little trinkets like pin-wheels and coins and an occasional poem. But after some time people move on, and then we're left to be forgotten—only remembered when some chump happens upon our stones and imagines what our lives had been. And maybe if we led a mysterious life or did some amazing feat, generations after may stand at the foot of our graves asking questions that cannot be answered. Maybe our time on Earth is to figure out how petty everything really is, and that things that bring us more pain than joy should be let go. How freeing would that be?

I neared the area of the cemetery where Wild Devil Jim and Eliza Morning Star rested and Dad was gone. At first I thought I was lost, that I had returned to the wrong area of the cemetery, but I checked the stones and I was in the right place. I looked to my left, to my right, behind me, and Dad had totally vanished.

"Dad!" I called out.

No response.

"Dad!" I called out, again, in another direction.

No response.

Well, god dammit!

I peeked behind bushes and large monuments. No luck. I continued to shout.

Somehow, he had completely disappeared. I started to think that maybe he had been abducted. And then I thought about the heat of the day, and Dad's age, and that he wasn't in the best shape of his life. What if he were on the ground? What if he'd had a heart attack?

I would sometimes forget that I was an adult and that my parents were aging, and in those moments I had to be the responsible party if something went wrong.

I hustled around the cemetery and looked in every possible hiding spot not visible to the naked eye. I continued to shout. Dad, simply put, was gone.

Off to the edge of the cemetery was a path that led out of the chain-link fence and into a wooded area. It was the only place I hadn't ventured, and I started to get a creepy feeling of what might be beyond the path.

Deranged hillbillies? Zombies? Zombie hillbillies?

I made my way down the path and thought each step I took could have been my last, and maybe had been Dad's too. The path opened up to a cleared area that allowed the sun to shine down upon a handful of newer looking head-stones. And there stood Dad, with his back to me, staring at someone's grave.

"Dad? Did you not hear me calling?"

He turned to me, startled. "Oh, sorry. No I didn't. How's Cory?"

I walked up to where he was. I looked at the headstone, taken in by what Dad observed. It was new, exceed-
ingly large, four feet tall and about four feet wide; black
marble with a picture of a teenage girl engraved in the
middle. I calculated the space between her birth date and
death date. *Sixteen.* A short story about her life was
carved near the bottom of the stone. She liked horses,
being a country girl, and she was taken too soon. Her
grave was only four years old. *Why would anyone bury her
here?*

I didn't answer Dad's question. I felt the tears beginning
to well up. I started to tremble.

"Must've been killed in a car wreck. Or cancer. Is Cory
doing all right?" Dad asked again.

I continued to stare at the headstone. "He's okay. We
have to put Sally down this evening. But don't worry, I'm
staying on the trip."

I hoped not making eye contact with Dad would have
kept me from crying in front of him, but the tears fell
anyhow. My chin quivered. I wasn't tough or brave.

Dad put his arm around my shoulders and pulled me in
tight for a hug. I felt the sweat from our shirts touch. He
kissed my head. "Everything that's born will die. I'll never
forget the day Dad told me he had to shoot old Smokey.
That was when I was away at Bible college. I almost
couldn't forgive him, but I had to move on."

He let go of me and walked toward the trail that led
back into the older part of the cemetery. I stayed at the grave
of the girl I didn't even know, in tears, not for her, but for the
loss of Sally, for trying to bond with Dad, to find our
common ground, and I wasn't even sure if it was possible

anymore. All I wanted was for him to not be so tough; to not move on so fast. Sally was my child. She wasn't *just* a dog.

Dad turned back only to motion for me to come on, and he suggested it was time for us to go. Dinner at the Rock Fair Tavern awaited us. And that was that.

I followed him out of the cemetery, four or five steps behind, because I didn't want to be left there and I had nowhere else I could go. We didn't even stop by Wild Devil Jim's and Eliza Morning Star's graves to say goodbye.

I almost couldn't forgive him for being so strong, so insensitive—for teaching me to be so strong and so insensitive. And maybe I was mad at myself because as hard as I practiced on stage and tried to play the role, the truth was I've never been able to perfect the part of a tough man who staves off his emotions. I've never been able to follow through with punching mother-fuckers right in the mouth.

I stumbled behind like a lost puppy and let out whimpers for all that had been left behind; the minutes and days and months and memories that all led up to that moment. Some of us have a funny way of dealing with loss. Some of us stay strong and practical, like Dad, and others, like me, fall apart. There was no in between. No space for common ground between a dad and a son.

THE THIRTY-MINUTE DRIVE from Sligo to Steelville seemed like an eternity. We decided to take a slightly different route to cut through Cherry Valley. A change of scenery, I supposed. Every few miles Dad said something along the lines of, "That's a shame about Sally," and then followed by, "You ready to get a beer at the Rock Fair tonight with your old dad?"

I answered with a "That's okay," followed by a "That sounds good."

I stared out the window to ignore Dad. No tears. Only silence, other than those short answers to his questions. This passive-aggressive positioning was a weapon I've used with my closest allies to get what I've wanted, and from Dad all I wanted to hear was an apology. An "I'm sorry for being insensitive," an "I'm sorry I think Donald Trump is great even though he hates people like you," an "I'm sorry for . . ."

I didn't really know what all I wanted Dad to apologize about. Even one "sorry" would have done the trick. Maybe I wanted him to apologize for convincing me to go on the trip; for always teaching me to be brave and to fight back, but never teaching me that it's okay to cry; for teaching me that it's not okay to admit I'd made mistakes in life. I needed a sorry for making me so tough on the outside that I ran from all of the feelings and emotions on the inside.

"Dad," I broke the silence. "What's flapping in that tree?"

Dad squinted his eyes. "Looks like some type of sheet."

As we neared closer, the white square panel was actually two sheets side by side tied between two towering oak trees. Spray painted in red and black on the one: DONALD TRUMP 4 PRESIDENT!!! On the other, also in red and black: MAKE AMERICA GRATE AGAIN!

Well, Jesus Fucking Christ they can't even spell.

I looked at Dad and laughed. "Well, that's the shittiest fucking homemade job I've ever seen, and this is your guy. A billionaire who is asking all of these poor motherfuckers to vote for him. Maybe he'll help them learn how to spell."

That bridge over our canyon of divide? I'd made it collapse.

Dad looked at me, equal parts of shock and pride. "Joe, these people around here are simple. They're not college-educated folks, and Trump speaks to them in a way that nobody else will. Hillary certainly doesn't speak to them." He let out a short laugh and shook his head as if to dismiss my comments and their spelling errors.

"He's definitely not their answer," I suggested and soon realized I had gotten the final word. Silence, again. My mind scaled the wall to find our bridge.

I thought about Silas and Rick and Leslie. They were good people who saw no hope in any other candidate or in the future of Missouri without Donald Trump. I recalled all of the Trump signs I'd seen dotted across the landscape of this state, along rural stretches of land headed to and from Cuba and Salem and Sligo all the way to the busy summer-time streets of Steelville with its weekenders floating down the Meramec. I remembered the Wisconsin couple from breakfast and them traversing the country, backward and forward, professing their love for the man who vied to be forty-fifth president of the United States.

Maybe he is their hope. But why can't it be somebody else? Like Hillary.

But Dad hated her. Supporting Hillary Clinton, to Dad, was basically like me saying to him, "I wanted all of your friends' jobs to go away." Ever since NAFTA passed in '94, Dad blamed the Clintons for our country becoming not so great—at least in his eyes, and I suspected in the eyes of all of those who chanted "Lock her up" while they wore those stupid *Make America Great Again* red hats. But at least the producers of those hats could spell.

"I'm voting for Hillary, Dad. If Bernie Sanders doesn't win the nomination."

It was as if everything he ever knew about me, or thought he knew, was out the window—left behind somewhere on that old country road. He took my coming out as gay with a grain of salt, but god forbid I vote for Hillary Fucking Clinton. I had never shared my support for her out loud. It was like coming out all over again, but this time there was no olive branch. Nowhere to run. Maybe *this* divide was the one that would really do us in.

"Joe, she let our own military be killed in Benghazi. She's not for the working man. She's against the 2nd Amendment. And what has she done for the gays?"

"Donald suddenly supports the gays?"

"He said on TV the other day that he loves the gays."

Really? Like that statement alone made him a champion for LGBTQ rights. Let's not mention everything he'd said about nominating Supreme Court Justices who would overturn marriage equality. Or calling Caitlyn Jenner a man.

I sighed. We were talking about Hillary, and deep down I knew her own positions on LGBTQ individuals had been flip-floppy over the years.

I changed tactics. "She doesn't want to take your guns, Dad."

"I don't trust her, Joe. We can't risk putting someone like her in office."

We went back and forth and on and on about whether or not Hillary would go to every home across the country and storm in with troops of pantsuit-wearing women to take each and every gun. I asked Dad if he thought AKs should be used for hunting, and he told me it'd obliterate a deer; that there's no real reason to shoot an animal with something like that. He laughed and then quickly cleared his throat to indicate he wasn't done debating. "It's a slippery slope if we start deciding who should be able to get a gun and what kind."

The truth was, I kind of agreed with Dad. As much as I loved animals and I wouldn't hunt, I also loved eating meat and knew that it took people like Dad, and guns, to make that a reality for me. But I didn't think assault rifles should be available to civilians, and I thought it was okay to do background checks on people who choose to buy a gun.

Only weeks earlier, Omar Mateen entered the Pulse Nightclub in Orlando, Florida, and opened fire, killing forty-nine people and wounding fifty-three others. All mostly LGBTQ folks like me. He sought them out and hunted them down. He studied the layout of the bar and determined where he could get the most kills. It was rumored that Mateen was closeted. That he had hid who he truly was deep within, under many layers of lies and truths. He had allowed the hate for himself to fester and boil up close to the surface. It waited to pop right through, and when it did, he didn't accept who he was. He took down those who were like him. The real him. He was afraid of the truth. Afraid of what the future held. When people are afraid, they make bad decisions. Decisions that can alter their futures. Decisions that make them stand behind men who would take them down if they didn't pass.

Dad told me we would need to agree to disagree. We fell into silence, again.

I had more in me. More truths I wanted to reveal. More issues I wanted to point out and then point out again to try to show him what was wrong with his beliefs on those issues. I thought about letting him know I had raised $4,000 the summer before to help relocate a Syrian family to the U.S. because Indiana's Governor, Mike Pence, decided not to allow any refugees into the state. The family had been slotted to arrive in Indianapolis the following week, but were instead redirected to Connecticut. The organization taking them in had no more funds to support the family, so I did what I felt like was the right thing—to show them *Hoosier Hospitality* and provide what I could to let them know that not everyone in Indiana is backward.

I wanted to point out that Mike Pence was rumored to be on Trump's list of V.P. candidates if he won the nomination, and that Pence had created the Religious Freedom and Restoration Act—also known as RFRA. RFRA was a license for religious communities to discriminate against the LGBTQ community. Suddenly, in Indiana, gay couples were turned away from bakeries and pizza parlors under the guise of religious freedom that was being expressed by their owners. Did he not understand how frightening it was for Cory and me to go out to eat during that time and not know if we would get turned away? *Straights Only.* What about Wild Devil Jim and Eliza Morning Star? Would Trump and Pence support their illicit love?

My urge to argue had surfaced again. But that wasn't going to prove anything to Dad other than to show how different we had become in our beliefs. He was right, agree to disagree. I wasn't going to sway him, and he wasn't going to sway me. That wasn't the path to common ground on the bridge above our divide. I knew what was.

I cleared my throat. "For the record, I don't like Hillary either. But I sure as hell ain't voting for Trump."

We stared out the window, in silence, at the land my ancestors settled upon for their own freedoms; to be who they were meant to be and to believe what they wanted. It was a land I understood, but one that no longer seemed familiar.

THE ROCK FAIR TAVERN sat close to the highway and looked like a massive pile of rocks with a door and a few windows. I guess maybe that's how it got its name. The bar opened in 1934 as a gas station but almost immediately its best seller changed from gas to beer, and soon after the place stopped selling gas altogether.

Grandpa Harrison wandered into the Rock Fair each night, slid up to the bar, and stayed until closing time. He ordered a Stag beer and told the bartender to keep them coming.

Dad was six the first time he had a drink at the Rock Fair. His dad sat him down on a barstool and said, "Bartender, get this kid a drink!" And now, some sixty-six years later, Dad said the same thing to the bartender about me. The only difference was that I was thirty years older than he was when he had his first drink at this place.

Grandpa Harrison's beer of choice was Stag before he switched over to whiskey and then vodka. Dad and Grandpa were never close. Most nights, Grandpa never came home. But one morning, he stumbled through the door smelling like the perfume of Rose Shreves. He leaned in to give Grandma Charlotte a kiss and she met his mouth with her fist. She knocked him back a few steps out the door until he lost his balance and fell to the gravel drive. He never came home smelling of perfume again; though it was rumored he fathered a child with Rose. He even gave the kid a job at the grocery store when he was a teenager. Dad, a teenager himself, stocked shelves next to him for no pay when Grandpa asked him to help out. The kid, only a couple of years younger than dad, eventually moved away from Steelville and started his own family in Arizona. Years later, Dad heard he had died from cancer.

When Dad told me this story, his voice cracked. Hands shaking, he pulled a black and white photo, creased down the middle, from his wallet; one he had carried with him for years. Two boys, Dad and this kid, stood shoulder to shoulder, one arm wrapped around each other, with the biggest smiles on their faces. They both wore long aprons, shelves of dried goods behind them. Dad pointed to the kid and asked me to examine their noses. They were, without a doubt, exactly the same. "I always knew he was my half-brother, but we never talked about it."

Grandma Charlotte knew, too, and she didn't like Dad hanging around this kid, and she definitely didn't like that Grandpa had given him a job at the grocery.

Part of me wondered why Dad wanted to come back to this place; to have a drink with me here at the bar that kept his Dad from him. But I took swigs of my Stag and glanced at the menu without questioning his motives. I had done enough questioning in my mind already.

I assumed Grandpa, as odd as it seemed, found those moments when he brought Dad to this bar as his way of bonding with his son; just as getting his other son a job at the grocery was the only place he could spend time with him. Both places where he could sneak the drink. And perhaps Dad felt this same bar provided a strengthened bond between the two of us. It wasn't our debate about politics that brought us there; Dad had talked about going to the Rock Fair long before we left for Missouri.

The old bar seemed to have a way with swiping all cares away.

Dad lifted his beer toward mine and we met in the middle, clinking our bottles together before chugging down what was left. Agree to disagree, or agree not to talk politics and enjoy that we have a shared history together at this bar, in this state, at this moment.

My text dinged: SHE'S GONE.

I looked at the clock on my phone and noticed it was almost 5:30. Cory had kept his promise to let me know. I didn't cry; I didn't even tell Dad who had texted. We finished our meal, paid our tab, and headed back to the motel where Dad said he'd like to spend the remainder of the evening relaxing in the air conditioning and watching TV. I knew that meant Fox News.

I told Dad something hadn't settled well with my stomach, so instead of laying on the bed watching talking heads and stewing over it all, I locked myself in the bathroom and let it all go.

Fearful tears—afraid of the future and my relationship with Dad.

Dad used to be my home, my rock, the man who always reached across any divide to let me know I was still his son. But I wasn't sure I knew how to find my way back to him. We all need certain things from certain people, and Dad couldn't offer what I needed in that moment. But my tears could. My weakness could.

Sometimes we need tears more than we need punches.

8

THE NEXT MORNING, the heaviness from the day before had been lifted overnight. I breathed better, I felt stronger.

I was alive.

Dad was already awake and sat on the edge of his bed. He stared at the TV, and I was certain it was Fox News . . . again. I'd come to believe it was one of the few channels available in the town.

I slid on my glasses and leaned forward. My eyes focused into view breaking news on the screen: BRITISH PM SAYS HE WILL STEP DOWN. UK VOTES TO LEAVE THE EU.

The referendum known as Brexit had passed by a narrow margin. Fifty-two percent in favor to forty-eight percent who opposed. Seventy-two percent of Brits showed up to the polls, but thirteen million of them stayed home. A victory?

I grabbed my phone and went to *The Guardian*, a British liberal-leaning news outlet; a trusted source that's far away from Fox News. Their editor-at-large, Gary Younge, reported: AFTER THIS VOTE THE UK IS DIMINISHED, OUR POLITICS POISONED.

In a matter of hours the Pound had plunged to a worth of $1.35, the lowest since 1985. People were panicked, and experts said the UK would go into a recession. Brits woke up in a country that didn't exist when they went to sleep the night before.

I thought: *Thank, God. Let's hope all of this bad news is a wake-up call to the American people.*

I mean, don't get me wrong, my love for the Brits has always been strong, and they make the best swimwear; it's hard to find three-inch inseam trunks in the States. But at least they were first, and I knew the fallout from their exit could teach us Americans a lesson. Then I remembered the divorce from the European Union could take two years to play out. The American system was always much faster.

Well, fuck, we're screwed.

I knew the Trump supporters would see this as a major victory and a sign for what could come in the U.S. And by what's to come I don't mean the negative—like a recession—I mean they'd see the independence of it all as a symbol of freedom.

I closed the browser for *The Guardian*.

The breaking news still scrolled at the bottom of the TV screen as the clip switched over to Donald Trump who was in Scotland for the re-opening of his golf resort, *Trump Turnberry*. News reporters from every outlet crowded around as wind whipped microphones and a band of bagpipes played in the background.

"Tell us what you think about Brexit," one reporter shouted.

Trump responded, "I think it's a great thing. They took back their country." And then he walked on to play his Scottish golf course.

The clip switched back to the Fox News newsroom and the talking heads who claimed the Brexit approval was a rejection of Barack Obama, who had campaigned for the UK to stay in the European Union. They argued from their right-wing viewpoint that this was a prophetic sign that voters would reject Obama's anti-Trump message in November during the presidential election. Donald Trump, they predicted, would be the next President of the United States.

I felt the sudden urge to vomit.

Dad leaned back on his bed and rested his weight on his elbows. He told me he thought Trump was probably right and that this would end up being a good thing. He ended it with a—"Yeah?"

A question at the end of a statement. An attempt to get me to agree.

I had decided the night before that agreeing to disagree was probably better, and accepting Dad for what he believed was in both of our best interests. But I was more awake than ever and I wasn't going to back down from my beliefs. It was time to push each other; to hold each other accountable.

I stood and stretched. "No, not really. I mean, there's excitement around it all, sure, but that doesn't mean it's good for the country. We'll see an impact here, too. If the ultimate goal is to prove a point by electing Trump and sending our country into a recession, we all need to get smarter. You know, stuffing our money into mattresses and shit. That'll really show them!"

Dad grinned and his eyes lit up, but he also shook his head. Like the day before, equal parts shock and pride. I wasn't serious. Well, at least not about hiding money. I had hoped he heard the sarcasm in my voice.

I stepped into the bathroom, closed the door, turned on the water and let it blast loudly as I dropped my boxers and stood naked in front of the mirror. I examined myself. My face. My crow's feet. My arms, dangled at my side. I turned them inward and let my triceps pop. I tightened my chest and watched my pecs bulge.

I was strong. I *could* punch mother-fuckers right in the mouth.

I lifted my arms and flexed my biceps. For all of the perceived weaknesses I'd ever felt—the pain of religion, my queerness, my identity, standing up against Dad—I felt stronger than ever.

I cracked a smile and began to laugh at the ridiculousness of standing, naked, in front of the mirror to prove my machismo to only me. But I needed to see it; to be reminded that everything that defines me is not a weakness but a strength. It was the courage I felt I needed to get through the next two days, and the following five months left until the election. I let my arms fall to my sides, I relaxed my face, and I saw not a boy but a man. A thirty-seven-year-old man. Strong but worn. Independent but woven with all of the fibers from his past.

A memory flashed before me of my senior year of high school, when I let my bravery come out, a little. A group of friends and I coordinated a senior skip day to go see the 20th anniversary re-release of *Star Wars*, and I had hemmed and hawed for a few days about whether or not I wanted to mess up the perfect attendance record I'd held since freshman year. But it was a chance to see the original *Star Wars* in the theatre, and it was my last chance to feel like I was breaking some rules before I left home for college and wouldn't have to ask for permission anymore. After much deliberation, and then eventually convincing Mom to call off school for me, I let the group know I was in.

We gathered that morning in the parking lot of a Hardee's; the harsh Indiana winter blew iced-wind with spits of snow into our faces. We made our plan for the day that included eating breakfast, driving to the big city of Muncie to hang out at the mall, seeing *Star Wars*, and then heading back to classmate's house in Cowan where we'd spend the rest of the afternoon. A perfect winter skip day for a bunch of seventeen year olds.

At Beth's house, her mom greeted us with fresh-baked chocolate chip cookies and homemade hot chocolate, the kind made on a stovetop in a stock pot. Her house smelled like a Christmas store; wafts of cinnamon and evergreen candles floated through the air. Beth's mom let us know she'd be upstairs reading if we needed anything, and left us to our own devices in the family room. This consisted mainly of gossiping while flipping through the latest SPIN and SEVENTEEN magazines. Beth painted her finger nails as we talked. She held one hand out in front of her to admire the midnight blue with silver sparkles before she moved on to her next hand. As she dipped the brush into the bottle her eyes caught mine and she noticed how I watched in admiration.

"I've never seen a color quite like that," I said.

"It's called Camaro Blue. Here, give me your hand."

After she painted my nails, I held both of my hands out in front of me and fluttered my fingers from side to side to allow the light to hit the sparkles. Nerves ripped through my stomach and sent tingles into my chest. If I left the nail polish on through the weekend, kids at school would see what I'd done come Monday. Though the nervous energy wasn't much about them. I was used to the "Hey, Gay-R" the boys would shout at me in the hallways. This would have only been more ammo for their typical cheap shots. I was nervous because I knew that after Beth's house, I had to go home. I could only hide my hands in my pockets for so long.

At the dinner table that evening, I let the Camaro Blue out in full force as I scooped chili from a bowl into my mouth. Mom and Dad didn't say a word. I mean, they asked about the skip day and what we did at Beth's house, but beyond the magazines and hot chocolate I didn't share much. I waited for one of them to ask about my nails, but it never happened.

That night, as I got ready for bed, Mom left a bottle of fingernail polish remover and a bundle of cotton balls on the bathroom counter. I picked up the bottle and examined the pink substance through the light, and then I put it back where I found it. The bottle and cotton balls were gone the next morning when I got up. I left my nails painted for two weeks. The Camaro Blue began to chip away around the edges and it was past time for a touch up. I went to the bathroom and found the fingernail polish remover and cotton balls in the closet. I scrubbed each nail until they were back to their old selves. I threw each Camaro Blue cotton ball into the trash, careful not to let them sink to the bottom but to stay on top, as a reminder to everyone who saw them in the Jamison household that I had done something without permission and I would not hide.

Several weeks later, on Easter Sunday, I woke to find a bottle of dark gray nail polish on my dresser with a note propped against its side. It wasn't a gift from Jesus or the Easter Bunny. The note read: *Love, Mom.*

I picked up the bottle and examined the contents. Small flecks of sparkle lay within the dark gray polish: *Take it for Granite.* I laughed at the name. I screwed off the top and took a whiff. I dipped the brush and brought my nails back to life, stroke by stroke. I never asked Mom why she thought of me when she saw the polish, or why she bought it for me —her son—or why she decided to leave it in my room without a mention other than the note. It went unspoken for years until Mom told me she'd always known I was gay. She said long before Dad ever found the letter from Steve; even though I'd waited another three years after Dad found out to let her know. He had suggested that night on the couch that maybe it would be best to keep the news between the two of us. He wasn't sure how she'd react. But "Mothers just know," she said. And she told me she always loved me and always will.

At the dinner table, my nails sparkled in the light as I brought forks and spoons from plates and bowls to my mouth. It wasn't until one Saturday, not long before I graduated from high school that Dad brought up my painted nails.

We were alone. An old Western played on the TV screen in the background, and Dad sat in his easy chair doing a crossword. Without looking up from the clues, he asked if other boys at school were doing the same.

"I don't know, Dad. Maybe."

He raised an eyebrow but kept his eyes on the puzzle. "These kinds of trends," he said, "they come and they go."

I graduated from high school wearing *Take it for Granite*, and each time my nails began to chip the remainder of that summer I'd touch them up with the bottle that was my very own.

I PULLED BACK the shower curtain in our room at the motel and stepped into the blasting water. It ran down my face, my neck, my chest, my thighs. Everything that needed to be cleansed ran down my legs and into the tub. A fresh start.

The continental breakfast wasn't any different than it had been the day before. Not even any protein to mix it up. I scanned over the options. I guess I imagined something new would appear the more I stared, but, alas, nothing did. Not even a make-your-own waffle station I had dreamed about each morning. I settled, again, on Cheerios and a slice of toasted wheat bread with Nutella. Coffee, black.

As Dad fixed up his heaping plate of biscuits and gravy, I approached the five wooden tables and noticed it wasn't as buzzing as the day before. The TV was on, and—you guessed it—Fox News was on the screen. The handful of folks in the room watched it—intently.

Dad parked his plate on the table and took the seat to

my right. Not to my left like he had the morning before. I chose the seat I was in with careful precision, under the assumption Dad would choose the seat to my left; thus, putting his back to these handful of folks in the room. But, not like how I'd planned, he had a perfect view of all of them and the TV. And there I sat in a moment of weakness. A thirty-seven year old man—who had minutes before stood in front of a mirror and reminded himself how strong he was —silenced, feeble.

I tried to channel my inner Wild Devil Jim and Eliza Morning Star. How would they have responded in this moment? Would they have been brave? Would they have joined in the conversation, or have been the ones to begin it so they could have controlled the narrative? I closed my eyes and transported myself back to Mr. Cochran's gym class. *Punch that son-of-a-bitch right in the mouth.* I could hear Dad's mantra in the back of my head. *Be strong. Be brave.*

And then it disappeared.

I opened my eyes.

It was so easy to become a boy again. Not one of the cool kids that hooted and hollered in the locker room, but the one who sits and doesn't speak. Back home I felt strong. I tried here, I did. But I had spent the last two days in the belly of an alternate reality. A place where everyone seemed to be under the hypnosis of Trump. Jobs, the economy—the only things they'd hear. Not racism or sexism or homophobia. Only class divides. Would nostalgia outweigh doing what's right? Would it cause these people—and Dad—not to stand up against fascism and instead choose unrealistic promises over other people's needs and concerns?

The truth was I didn't fit in there. As much as I wanted

to rediscover my roots—my hillbilly roots—and find a connection back to Dad and learn what had separated us, I still sat at that breakfast table and wore my *Cartier Love* bracelet—that sparkled in the drop-ceiling lights—as I scrolled through my iPhone 6S. I was an outsider. I was a stranger in a strange land, but if I sat really still maybe I could fit right in. Perhaps that's the danger of being different but looking like everybody else.

But those handful of people who sat around the TV weren't really into discussion. Dad didn't even entertain them. He sat there, tilted his head to the left and to the right, turned his fork sideways and sliced into his biscuits and gravy. *Hmmphs* between bites. It was only us, Trump, and Rhonda who still stood behind the counter waiting to check guests into the motel. The same routine. Day after day. The breakfast, the table, the TV, the conversation. Only the people had changed. And since these people were quiet, and so was Dad, I'd gotten my alone time, figuratively.

And since my wishes seemed to work, I closed my eyes again and wished to be back home. A place where Sally was still alive. A place where all my friends thought like me and we poked fun at the simple minds who had professed their love for Donald Trump. A place where I had a voice and wasn't worried what Dad thought about my viewpoints and the way I saw the world. But that place, too, was an alternate reality. Group think. No one in, no one out. A place where we held our own prejudices against people like Dad, and we could get away with it.

The truth was, as much as I didn't want people pre-judging me for being queer, I knew it wasn't fair for me to judge the people I had encountered on Dad's turf. It was easy to paint them with a broad brush, but I don't like it when people do that to people like me.

I opened my eyes and focused my attention on the food before me. Cheerios and Nutella toast never tasted so good. I'd stopped listening to the voices in my head, and all of the energy it took to listen shifted to my taste and smell. I've always heard that a deficit in one of the senses increases the others. And I could sense the Nutella was old.

Every now and then my sense of sound came back as Rhonda echoed from afar in her gruff voice, "Thanks for calling. Please hold." Then I immediately focused my attention back to my sense of taste and the stale but sugary mixture in my mouth.

Dad squeezed my knee. "Let's top off our coffees and hit the road for Steelville."

He explained that, even though we'd be back in Steelville that evening for his high school reunion, he wanted to go that way now to visit Old Lady Baker, and we could come back to the motel later on to get freshened up before the big night.

I told him I needed a minute and that he could go on and get freshened up now if he wanted, because I had to touch base with Rhonda to make sure we were all set with check out for the next morning. Really, though, I needed Rhonda's advice. As crass as she seemed, I'd actually snuck to the lobby a few times on the trip to seek her guidance. She was someone who was direct and told it like it was. She reminded me of Mom—someone who understood someone like Dad—and something about her candidness comforted me.

I met Rhonda at the counter. She wasn't smiling, and I

detected wafts of cigarette smoke filling the space around her. I knew I'd caught her at the right time.

"What'll it be today?" she said.

I stared at the counter.

"You know, it's really great you traveled back here with your dad to attend his reunion. Are you excited about it?"

"I guess. I mean, maybe I'm a little nervous," I said.

"Don't be. Cherish these moments."

"I'm trying, it's just the way we each approach situations is different. I sometimes get frustrated—"

"Don't. Not everybody gets these types of chances with their dad. My dad used to annoy the crap out of me, but if I could go back I'd spend time with him every chance I got."

"I get it. I do. It's just sometimes hard to remember that because we are so different."

Rhonda's face dropped. It was her not-so-subtle way to let me know her free advice for the day had expired. And then she disappeared again somewhere in the back.

That was okay because I heard a song playing softly from the motel sound system that was going to make me let loose. Make the real me come out right there in the lobby. Madonna's *Holiday*.

The beat . . . *dun-ta-dun—dun-ta-dun—dun-ta-dun—dah!*

I felt the unspeakable coming on right then and there. I wasn't sure I could resist. Arm swing, back and forth, up above the head, now down to the floor. I thought about that ruffle-y, polka-dotted number Madonna wore in the music video for her LIVE performance in Nice, France, and I imagined being dressed in it as I twirled in the lobby right next to the overstuffed floral couch and the continental breakfast. In my imagination Rhonda came back out and I spun her around, turning her into a tornado of smoke. But instead, I bobbed my head and walked on to the door that lead to the parking lot and to our room, Madonna singing in my ear.

9

OLD LADY BAKER lived on top of a hill on the way to Steelville but not quite in the city limits. The highway to her house was an old one that had been replaced with a newer one at the base of the hill. She went to high school with Grandpa Harrison, and he later hired her to work at his grocery. She kept the books and came once a week to pound her forefingers into the adding machine, pulling the lever to reveal the gains and losses. She was one of Grandpa Harrison's closest friends from his teen years. A friendship that always remained strictly platonic.

Old Lady Baker knew the stories of Grandpa before he took to the bottle; the high school days in the band, when he worked in the evenings at the brewery outside of town sweeping the floors to earn a few bucks to pay for the things his parents couldn't afford. Some nights, when the brewery had a bad week, they paid him in drinks rather than cash. He was a sixteen-year-old boy who stumbled home under the cover of darkness through the streets of Steelville, playing off his hangover in band practice the next day. Old Lady Baker reminded him that he didn't have to take the liquid payment, and in moments of pride he wouldn't. She stood by his side through growing up, marriage, family, and opening the grocery. She sat in the back room beyond the shelves of dried goods and counted the losses. In the room, she talked to Dad about Grandpa Harrison, and told him stories about his dad's days before the bottle. She helped Dad calculate the missing pieces of a father who was sometimes subtracted from the present equation, and she gave hope that people are more than what they show on the surface.

The back of Old Lady Baker's house was visible from where Dad put our car into park, along a gravel drive that led to a barn and access road for a soybean field. An old farm dog circled us and barked up a storm. The silhouette of a person on the screened-in back porch made it obvious someone was home, but they weren't coming out.

Dad laid on the horn. One long blow, then a few short *beep-beep-beeps* followed by another long blow.

The screen door to the back porch creaked open and then it slammed shut. This repeated itself three times. With each episode, nothing happened. No one came out.

I saw the shape of a figure through the screen when the door popped open for a fourth time, but this go-round a cane poked out and stopped the door from slamming shut. Little by little—a foot, a leg, an arm—a whole person emerged.

"That's her. That's her!" Dad shouted. He rolled down my window and hollered at her. "Mrs. Baker!"

"Oh," she screeched out, "don't you worry about Rufus. He won't bite." She came to my window and steadied herself against the door, peering inside to give Dad a good look. "Little Davey Jamison," she said to him in a voice that sounded like an out-of-tune violin. "I figured I'd be seeing you. It's the reunion tonight, ain't it?"

"It sure is." Dad's eyes grew wide. "You going?"

"No, no!" She laughed. "I'm much too old to be getting out like that. Anyway, it'll be way past my bed time, and it's not *my* reunion. You boys wouldn't know what to do with an old woman like me. Why don't you turn off your car and come in and sit a spell."

Rufus ceased barking and sat at her side. As I got out of the car I reached down and allowed him to smell my hands before I rubbed his head and scratched behind his ears. We slowly followed her lead to the back porch. Dad stepped up beside her and tried to take her arm to help her along, but she refused and said she was only using a cane while she recovered from hip surgery.

"My goal is to not use this thing forever. I'm only ninety-seven. I ain't giving up yet."

Dad stepped back and walked behind her, along with Rufus and me.

"Can I offer you boys some iced tea?"

I wanted to say no because I didn't want to burden the poor old woman, but I was really thirsty and southern sweet tea sounded excellent. Besides, she seemed fiery and wanted reasons to not give up. If getting iced tea for us was one reason to keep going, then so be it.

Dad settled in on an old olive green and white steel porch glider.

I followed Old Lady Baker into the back of the house and helped with the tea.

"You probably wondered who this is," Dad said pointing toward me as I handed him his tea. "Well, this is my boy, J.R."

"You don't say!" She gave me a wink. "Of course I knew it was your boy, Davey. He looks just like you and just like Harrison."

I never met Grandpa Harrison. He finally drank himself to death when he was fifty-one. I've only seen one picture of him. The only picture Dad owned of him, and it was taken around 1940 when Grandpa and Grandma Charlotte got married. I have no idea of his personality other than hearing people say he was a drunk. Dad never shared many stories about him. But any time I have a little too much to drink, I always think about Grandpa Harrison and silently hope it doesn't overtake me someday as well.

We sipped our tea. The porch glider whistled in the background. Dad and Old Lady Baker made eye contact, and she tilted her head downward and smiled and then turned her attention to me. She asked if I wanted to hear some stories about Grandpa Harrison. I nodded.

She clapped her hands together with a laugh and then rested them on her knees. She leaned forward. "Your Grandpa was an excellent drummer. I played the drums right alongside him. He wasn't better than me, but he sure did beat all the other boys!"

She relished in the opportunity to share a few memories with us about him. About how he played pranks on other boys in the band. About the time when he poured water down the saxophones, where it rested in the bells and stopped the sound, and he replaced the reeds with chewing gum. As these discoveries were found, he pounded away on his snare and cracked a smile; his drumsticks floated up and down from the pocket of his thumbs and forefingers. Little jokes here and there to keep the rhythm of life moving forward.

With each word from Old Lady Baker I realized how ornery he was—like Dad and his fake marriage, or blowing up the quad hoping for a laugh. I guess the apple really doesn't fall far from the tree.

Old Lady Baker's tone became somber. She looked to the ground. "But the spring of '42 got the best of him. He never recovered from being rejected by the Army."

Grandpa Harrison tried to enlist not long after Pearl Harbor like many of the other men around Steelville had done, but partial blindness in his right eye made the Army give him a pass. During the war, sales at the grocery store were down and they never did bounce back. While his high school friends died across the ocean in places he'd only read about in books, he tried to figure out how to make ends meet for his new family. When the pieces hadn't come together, what he found was solace in the liquid courage that had been given to him as a kid at the brewery.

Old Lady Baker reached across the porch glider and grabbed Dad's hand. "Harrison sure did love his boys." She rubbed her thumb across the top and smiled at Dad. "He wanted the best for you, Davey, and he had hoped to get sober. You know that. I've told you before. He never could tell you, so I'm here to always remind you."

The whistle from the porch glider stopped. Dad wiped a tear from his eye and exhaled loudly, took a sip of his tea, and our eyes caught. He smiled but I could see the pain behind it. The whistle from the porch glider began again. "I loved him, too," Dad said.

A Dad and a son who never learned how to connect. They lived in the periphery of one another's lives but never met in the middle.

I always thought of Grandpa Harrison as a one-dimensional character. The town drunk. An embarrassment. But the truth is that we all are deeper stories than what is presented on the surface. We are more than the pain we've caused or the narratives we've tried to create for those who want to look inside. I've known this for some time. It's why I founded The Facing Project and have spent my career trying to connect people across difference. I need, and want, people to recognize the human condition, but sometimes it's hard to see, to feel, to understand the stories of those closest to us. Perhaps it's a fear of being let down, and a fear of accepting truths that we don't want to embrace.

Grandpa Harrison may have been a drunk, but he was also a hurt man who didn't know how to cope with his mistakes and his shortcomings. The hole he had created around himself kept getting deeper and deeper.

Dad may have moved to Indiana to run from his own failures and that of his dad's, and I may have run from the life that he tried to create for me in Cowan, but our stories—our past—*that* is home.

Old Lady Baker said her class hadn't had a reunion in years. "Primarily because most of them are gone."

Something about that sent sadness to my heart. There she was, an amazingly spry and healthy ninety-seven year old, the kind of old that makes you stop and think: *I hope I live to be ninety-seven and my life is like hers.*

But then I remembered if I make it that long, most of the people I've loved will no longer be there to celebrate it with me. What must that be like? My mind shifted to Steve. The pain of that loss was still deep. I imagined it would be like that but magnified a dozen times over. And I thought about Dad. If I lived to be ninety-seven, he would be one-hundred-and-thirty-three. Long gone. Cory and I likely won't ever have kids. *Who will be there when I'm ninety-seven?*

I worry about dying alone in a nursing home without any kids of my own. *Will Wild Devil Jim's and Eliza Morning Star's rebel-hearts end with me?*

I wanted kids at one point. I thought I'd make a good dad. Cory never wanted to get married or have kids. After we dated for some time, we entered the *where-are-we-going-next* phase of our relationship, and I took a risk and told him I wanted to get married. He resisted at first but one fall morning, several months later, as we lay in bed with Alton Brown's *Good Eats* in the background, Cory asked me to marry him. "Maybe this summer," he said. "But don't go pressuring me to have kids." And that was our engagement.

It may not seem super sweet, but it was perfect to me. And we had our commitment ceremony that following summer. Each time we had to get remarried because of the ever-shifting laws of our state and the country, I promised him I wouldn't pressure him to have kids as long as he married me. I never have.

In the back of my mind, I've always thought that some-how, some way, I'd be a dad someday. I'd name my boy Harold Clyde. I'd call him Harry for short, a nod to Cory's Grandpa Harold and to my own Grandpa Harrison. I guess I've given it more than a few thoughts. The older I get, the more I see this fictional kid fading away. And the more I worry about my legacy and what will happen to me when I'm old, like Old Lady Baker. Grandpa Harrison tried to right a wrong with Dad but never quite did. I may never have kids, but maybe I could've made things right with my own Dad before it was too late for us.

The heaviness of those thoughts was more than I could bare. I closed my eyes to center myself again. A warm summer breeze made the wind chimes clang in a stuttered rhythm. I sipped my iced tea and took it all in with no words to add.

I thought about everything Old Lady Baker had seen in her lifetime.

The Great Depression. The New Deal. World War II. Nazis. The economic boom of the 50s. The creation of the Interstate system. Chauvinistic men. Girl Fridays. The Vietnam War. Hippies. Women's Lib. The first human on the moon. Watergate. Solar power. The Religious Right. Reaganomics. The War on Drugs. The Clintons. Monica and the Impeachment. The Internet. 9/11. The War on Terror. The first Black president. ISIS. Marriage Equality. And, now, the chance for the first woman president amidst the rise of Donald Trump.

All that and she was still there, smiling. As if nothing beyond the screened-in porch mattered. It gave me hope for enduring the impossibility of a Trump presidency. But of course, I wondered what her secret was. Was she this at ease with herself because she was ninety-seven? At what point had she stopped caring about the negativity—all of the endless news cycles—and decided to live her life for her? And, of course, for Rufus.

Will I ever reach that point? Should I reach that point? Is that what being brave truly is? Letting it all go?

The truth was, Old Lady Baker *was* the resistance. She had persevered through all of history that had been stacked up against women. She rolled up her sleeves and held down the fort when Grandpa Harrison's business was failing, and she remained in Dad's life throughout all of these years to remind him that his dad, indeed, loved him. She didn't have to do any of those things, but she did because setting the future on the right path was important to her. And through it all, she taught me that relaxing on a porch isn't giving up or not caring. Stepping away from it all for a minute is a reminder that there are more important things in life than the noise of the day; more than the narratives we manufacture in our heads about each other; and more than party or belief.

Old Lady Baker was a reminder that the simple things in life persist, even through the dark days, because the bright spots that come along are enough to keep going. They become reflections of hope and reminders that we all share the same human condition. If Old Lady Baker could show Dad that his dad did care, maybe her lessons could show me that the divides between Dad and me could be bridged.

We stayed at Old Lady Baker's for over two hours. Our conversation bounced from days gone by back to the reunion. Every now and then Rufus moved from me to her. She scratched his head and talked to him in a baby voice, and then she went back down memory lane as Rufus landed at my feet.

There was no talk of politics, not even once. No TV. No Fox News. No debates.

Those two hours were a retreat. A well-needed escape back to a time when nothing else mattered but the moment. Politics often feel vitally important in our time, but discussion of them is never a memory that sticks with anyone. Not like the way I knew I would remember sitting on that screened-in porch with that remarkable old woman and Dad, sipping iced tea, and learning a little more about his past and what ultimately created me.

Before we left, Old Lady Baker cupped Dad's hands in hers and shook them. Her eyes went from Dad to me and back again. "When our time comes, our time comes. But our stories are what matter. They're the only thing we got in the end."

Dad and I said goodbye to Old Lady Baker. He knew this was the last time he'd see her; the last time he'd have a living connection back to his dad.

10

"Is THIS THING ON STRAIGHT?" Dad tugged at his tie in the mirror. I stood beside him, rubbing styling paste between my palms and then through my hair. We spoke to each other's reflections.

"It looks straight to me, Dad, but it's a little short. You might need to re-tie it."

"Oh, to hell with it, I ain't wearing this stupid thing. I don't need to wear a tie do I?"

"Well, I'm not wearing one. That's for sure. So I'd say you're safe going without."

"If your mom was here she'd make me wear it."

"Well, I ain't Mom and your secret is safe with me."

Dad slid the knot down and pulled the tie over his head. He gave it a toss and it landed on top of his bag outside of the bathroom door. He undid the top button of his shirt and then untucked it from his pants. His shirt was unusually large and hung down almost mid-thigh.

"I think I'm gonna wear this thing untucked, too, huh?"

I grimaced. I certainly didn't get my sense of fashion from Dad. "I think you should probably tuck it in. It'll look a lot better."

Dad tucked his shirt back in and I finished messing with my hair. We stood in front of the mirror and stared at each other.

"If we was single men, we'd be breaking a lot of hearts tonight," Dad said with an unbridled laugh. He slapped me on the back and then left the mirror.

I stayed for a moment and stared at myself. I didn't flex my triceps. I didn't lift my arms to admire my biceps. I didn't even bounce my pecs. I had nothing left to prove to myself about my own strength. It was Dad's night, his reunion, and I decided to live in the moment and not get lost in all of our differences.

But I was nervous. I'd heard stories all my life about some of the people I would meet.

Would I be rendered silent, again? What if someone asked me about me? Is it okay to be truthful or should I just smile and let them decide who I am?

So many questions ran through my head. More than anything, I wanted Dad to feel proud of me but at the same time respected by his classmates. Based on the Trump signs that dotted the landscape, and the many conversations I'd encountered about Trump since we arrived, I had no other reason but to believe that most of Dad's old classmates would be opposite of me.

I smiled at myself in the mirror. I didn't excel at basketball or track like Dad, and I didn't spend my time in high school chasing the girls down Main Street, but I did spend my high school years becoming me. And that was something to be proud of and something I could hold onto as I met Dad's classmates.

A few years after I stood on the stage at Cowan, Dad and I attended a basketball game together. I sat a few feet from him, and I overhead him tell another dad, whose son scored shot after shot on the floor, "He's not really a sports guy, but he's one hell of an actor." He reached back to where I sat and squeezed my knee.

STEELVILLE HIGH WAS LOCATED on the outskirts of town, heading toward Cherry Valley. The parking lot stretched twice the length of the school, and on the night of the reunion most of the vehicles were clustered along the drive closest to the entrance to the building.

Dad parked as far away as possible, where the lot abruptly ended into a wooded area. He indicated it'd be easier to get out when we needed to leave and we wouldn't have to fight traffic. I didn't think the twenty or so vehicles would cause a jam, but I agreed with a nod.

Dad pulled down his visor, opened the mirror, and straightened his hair with his hand. "Welp, this is it. You ready?"

"Ready as I'll ever be!"

A nervous feeling tickled my stomach. The kind where you aren't sure if you need to poop or puke. Maybe both.

As we neared the entrance to the school I straightened my posture and gave myself a mental pep talk: *You are a talented person. You've done a lot of good in the world. These people will like you. Just be yourself.*

Dad put his arm around my shoulders and pulled me close to him as we entered. The smell of old books, pencils, and floor wax took me right back to Cowan High School. A place that held good memories but painful ones as well. I felt fifteen all over again. The deodorant canister barreled my way as Jacob shouted "faggot." The pain from the slate table bounced through my head. *Will these people accept me if I'm the real me?*

Dad once told me about a guy named Jerry Cagney and his son, Gary, who were both queer. They used to sneak over to the Rolla School of Mines to peek into the guy's windows in the dorm. Gary was around Dad's age, and Dad said Gary was like free entertainment. He sashayed his way down the hallway in his saddle oxfords, hand on his hip, a baby blue cardigan wrapped around his shoulders. He lisped his words with excitement and fluttered his hands to accentuate whatever point he made. Jerry was equally as flamboyant. "Poor Mrs. Cagney. How she didn't know is beyond me," Dad recalled.

Gary Cagney got stuffed into trash cans, his head whirled in toilets, but he got back up and walked down the hall with it held up high; albeit with gum on his back or hair sopping wet. Lining the halls, the jocks snickered and flipped rubber bands at him as he walked by.

Dad pulled his letterman jacket from his locker, slammed the door shut and told the other guys to knock it off. They fake upper-punched each other and performed headlocks as they walked to the lunch room to discuss the big game and their tactics to beat Bourbon that night. Dad told them how he almost went all the way with Lila, sitting in the cab of his truck on the side of the country road that led out to Cuba. Hands up her shirt and cupped on her breasts, they tongue-kissed under broken moonlight that filtered through windows. Two silhouettes that only made it to second base. The guys beat the table with the palms of their hands and howled like coyotes, encouraging future teen antics.

Will they accept me? Mental pep talk. Mental pep talk.

The entry area of the school was crowded with graduates from the classes of '56, '61, and '66. Each celebrating 60, 55, and 50 years out of high school. They stood in groups of threes and fours, falling into their cliques from all of those years ago. A registration table with the "HELLO, My Name Is" tags sat off in the corner. It was staffed by a man about my age, who I would later learn was the school's current principal. He welcomed each alum with a firm handshake and a big smile.

I immediately noticed how small everything was. Much smaller than Cowan and my whopping class size of forty-one. That gave me a boost of confidence. *I got this.*

I stood even taller. I wrote, *J.R. Jamison, son of Dave*, on my nametag, peeled it, and slapped it above my left nipple.

"Over there," Dad pointed. "I want you to meet somebody."

A man, much older than all the rest, was dressed in a Scout uniform and had a crowd of men around him. Dad weaseled his way through and put three fingers to his forehead.

"On my honor I will do my best to do my duty to God and my country and to obey the Scout Law; to help other people at all times; to keep myself physically strong, mentally awake, and morally straight."

Morally straight.

Those two words have always sent a chill down my spine. But Dad loved the Boy Scouts. They taught him how to grow from a boy to a man, and they helped him find a brother in James Pershing. He quit shy of earning his Eagle. One thing he's often said he regretted doing. I was no Boy Scout. Hell, I didn't even make it out of Tiger Cubs. The Boy Scouts have always reminded me that there are groups who actively hate the gays. I guess the bad taste in my mouth for the Scouts started at an early age.

One of the first moments I realized I wasn't like the other boys was when I was six. It was near Christmas. I helped Mom prepare crafts in anticipation of my fellow Tiger Cubs arriving for a den meeting. She and I filled paper plates with glitter, we sorted pipe cleaners into piles of brown, red, and green, and we placed each into assembling stations along the countertops in the kitchen. All of the den mothers were required to host a meeting at each of their homes, and this was our turn.

Each boy piled into the house and created a ruckus that spilled into the kitchen. Mom encouraged me to take everyone upstairs to play while she finished setting up the craft stations. Before the last sentence fell from her lips, we were halfway up the stairs squealing and pinching and laughing. The stream of Tiger Cubs before me ran directly to my room, when a sudden stop forced us into one another.

Immediate quietness.

Then a stocky, raspy-voiced boy named Brian, who stood at the lead, spoke first. "Why . . . do you . . . have so many . . . *dolls* . . . on your bed?"

I stared in silence, my eyes darted between Brian and

the dolls perfectly arranged: Rainbow Brite next to Teddy Ruxpin who sat next to My Buddy who strategically lay next to Robert, my adopted Cabbage Patch, all leaned against the next—Pinocchio, Lemon Meringue, Koosa Cat. Each doll stared back as if I had planned to abandon them. I looked at all of my fellow Tiger Cubs, each with his mouth open.

"Are you gay or something?" Brian questioned.

It was the first time that had been asked of me and I didn't know what to say. I was only six, and I didn't understand why all the other boys thought that the things I loved were wrong.

I quit the Tiger Cubs a couple of months later.

In college, Andrew, the guy Steve said was no good for me, was an Eagle Scout. His internalized homophobia was a little more than I could handle. He spent nights yelling at me and shamed both of us for being queer. He grew rattled whenever I tried to hold his hand in public. He made us "de-fag" our apartment before his parents came over. I guess I equated all of his behaviors to his years of having a "morally straight" code beaten into him day after day.

At the same time, James Dale—an Eagle Scout and Scoutmaster from New Jersey—made national headlines for challenging the Boy Scouts of America for revoking his Eagle and removing him from his post because it was discovered he was a gay man. The case made it all the way to the Supreme Court where they ruled the Boy Scouts had a right to ban gays from being involved in the organization.

All of these things, these memories, had soured my opinion of the Boy Scouts, even though they'd made strides in the last few years to welcome LGBTQ members and leaders. It took people like James Dale, who never gave up the fight, to be brave enough to step forward for these changes to eventually happen.

I still imagined a bit of homophobia and straight-centric society existed as a norm in the organization, especially among those who belonged years and years ago. But Dad took on the presence of a child in front of Scout Master Earl, and even though he hadn't been a Scout for nearly fifty-five years he still wanted to show respect for everything Earl had been to him. And the crowd of men who gathered around had the same admiration. That I *could* respect. It was not my place, or my time, to pass my thoughts, feelings, or judgements into their space. Sometimes it's better to listen than it is to speak *my truth* in the moment. Bridging divides takes listening as much as it does speaking.

I watched Dad recite the Scout's Oath, with his three fingers at his forehead, and, as much as I hated to admit this, it left me with a different feeling about the Scouts. This was Earl, the man who helped Dad perfect his jump shot. The man who was there all the times my Grandpa Harrison was not.

I made my way through the men and Dad introduced me to Earl. I told him it was quite the honor to meet him. I had the sudden urge to throw my three fingers up to my forehead and state the Scout's Oath. I even thought about giving it a try, but I knew I'd butcher it. He'd know I was a fake for sure.

"Are you a Scout, Son?" Earl asked.

"No, sir. I was more into theatre." I gulped. *What the hell am I saying?*

"Theatre? Well, your Dad here was one of the finest Scouts I ever had."

Dad immediately recalled the story about the first time Earl took all the boys on an overnight camping excursion where they had to pretend like they were lost in the wilderness. Dad howled. "Remember how a group of us hid the flares from the other guys?"

A few of the other men circled around and added in "Yeahs" and "Boy that was a night!"

Earl had a proud smile on his face and kept nodding without saying a word. He watched these men, who were once boys he helped raise, and I understood what it must be like to be a father; to see reflections of yourself all these years later, even if I would never experience that pride and wonderment myself.

Dad gave Earl a big bear hug and then we parted through the men. I turned to Dad, put my hands into my pockets, shrugged my shoulders, and cracked a smile. I hoped I hadn't embarrassed him too much. Dad rubbed the back of my head and put his arm around my shoulders. I did the same with my arm, and we walked into the gymnasium shoulder to shoulder. Dad and son.

Pennants of old sport's records danced above our heads. Long tables filled with chairs lined the floor from wall to wall. The backboards on either side of the gym were raised. It was the place where Dad had become a basketball star. The place where all the locals came out to watch Steelville beat Bourbon and all the boys became celebrities, at least for a night.

Dad spotted a few of his classmates from '61 at one of the tables and suggested we sit with them. He took a seat, and I settled in on his other side and hoped that none of the conversations would lead to politics.

Other classmates began to file in and took seats around us. A woman, dressed in so much pink she looked like an Azalea bush, introduced herself as Lillian. She was friendly and continually told me how handsome I was, and that I was a carbon copy of Dad. Another classmate, attending the reunion with his son from Texas, scooted up to the table in his motorized wheelchair. He parked at the table in the spot directly across from me.

We ate our dinners of fried chicken, mashed potatoes, and green beans served up on assorted colored cafeteria trays. The son from Texas made eye contact a few times, as if to say: *Can you believe we're here with this crew?* Stolen looks of solidarity, but we said few words.

During a break in the conversation, the table fell silent as everybody poked at their food and considered what to say next. Lillian turned her attention back to me. "So, J.R., I see that you're wearing a wedding ring. What does your wife do?"

I cleared my throat and hesitated.

Should I be honest and true to myself?

Will my truth cause Dad to lose his standing among this group?

Why is everyone staring at me?

My heart pounded and I felt sweat permeating the surface of my skin. Their eyes upon me felt like a thousand stares, the silence seemed like hours. I was a deer, and Dad's classmates were a pack of hunters. Earl sat a few chairs down.

"I'm not married to a woman. My husband works in healthcare."

Dad grabbed my knee and gave it a squeeze.

"Oh!" Lillian responded.

The other classmates continued to stare.

The man in the motorized wheelchair was startled by the news. His hand thrust forward and put his chair into overdrive—right through the table.

"Look out!" Dad yelled.

The table was knocked out of line and my tray of food balanced on the edge. Dad moved in the nick of time and saved himself from wearing his drink.

I began to giggle. The giggles became louder and barreled out of my chest as roars of laughter. Dad followed and we stood, doubled over. Laughter from Lillian began to boil up and, like a contagion, everyone near the table began to laugh; including the man who had almost run us over. His son from Texas didn't laugh. Earl, at least, cracked a smile.

I pushed the table back into place as Dad gathered napkins to sop up the puddle on the floor. We took our places back at the table.

Dad pointed at the motorized wheelchair. "Make sure that thing is in park."

"Now that everything is out in the open," I said to the table, "tell me more about all of you."

I was proud that I'd been true to myself—to who I was and why I was here. I wore that pride in the form of a smile as I listened to Lillian share stories about her trips across the country visiting the Grand Canyon, taking in the waterfalls of the southeast, and hiking trails in national parks. Another classmate talked about cattle ranching. Another spoke of now grown grandkids and their achievements.

The principal gave out an award for who traveled the farthest to get to the reunion. Dad won. A couple of guys patted him on the back as he walked to the podium and accepted his certificate. I gave him a thumbs up as he walked back.

Dad leaned in and asked everyone about the night Steelville beat Bourbon. "Remember who scored 40 points and got us that victory?"

"Denny Connor? Boy, he was an All-Star," a guy nearby replied.

Dad shook his head. "No. *No!* It was me!"

That was Dad's one moment of victory there in that little town. So many things in life had taken Dad far from there and far from the night when he was the star. No one else remembered, but it was Dad's time to set the record straight. He continued telling the story without missing another beat. Eyes widened with *oohhs* and *aahhs* as each person was taken back to that night through Dad's words.

I watched with admiration and discovery. A side of Dad I'd always known but had forgotten how to appreciate. Such a great storyteller. He had their undivided attention. Hours earlier, I'd told Rhonda I was embarrassed by Dad. But I guess I've always enjoyed his stories, even when I pretended I was too busy to listen. I'd always thought Dad's stories were overly nostalgic and repetitive, but the trip showed me what I'd guessed he'd tried to get through all along—sometimes one has to go back to find their true selves.

. . .

TOWARD THE END of the reunion Dad spotted James Pershing on the opposite end of the gymnasium from where we sat. He had a line of classmates before him, and stacked to his side was a pyramid of his book.

"There's that old fart. I wondered if he was coming. I'll be right back."

Dad didn't invite me to join him, and I didn't ask to go. I stayed behind and watched from afar as he waited in line to meet his old friend. *His brother.*

Lillian tried to make conversation with me again, and I pretended to listen as she continued, but my attention stayed on Dad. I watched as he became almost childlike once again. Something I saw him do with Earl. He eagerly awaited the moment he'd get to talk to James and to get his autograph.

Person after person, James struck a sharpie across the inside pages of the books and then handed them off with a few words and an occasional picture. When it was Dad's turn, he and James looked each other in the eyes and then embraced. They pulled back from each other, still holding on at the shoulders, and smiled. I could see their lips move, but I couldn't make out what they said.

James took a seat, grabbed a book, and began to write something. He handed it off to Dad and stood once again for a final hug and then a long handshake. Dad's smile and his eyes were the brightest I'd ever seen them. Lila, our family history, politics, the night he beat Bourbon, none of these had made Dad's eyes smile quite like this. James was his first friend. The guy who got him out of the house when Grandpa would come home too drunk. James had now become all of the successful things Dad thought he would become one day.

I felt like a jerk.

I'd made fun of James's book at the bank. I rolled my eyes in my mind at Mary Jane as she talked about James being at the reunion; about how he would sign books there like he was some hotshot whose memoir was a *New York Times* bestseller. I *pfft'ed* when I learned it was a story about death, rebirth, and Jesus. But it was a book so many of those people needed and wanted. Including Dad. Who was I to cut it down and tell them otherwise?

Dad returned to our table and opened the book long enough for me to see a paragraph of black scribbles. I was curious to know what James wrote, but instead of grabbing the book and peering inside I told Dad I couldn't wait to hear all about it after he read it.

One by one, Dad's classmates said their goodbyes and walked out of the gymnasium and back to their lives. Some of them, I imagined, wouldn't be back. The man from Texas hit another table as he tried to steer his motorized wheelchair away.

"Watch where you drive that thing!" Dad shouted with a laugh.

We were the last to leave. It's like Dad didn't want to go. He had nowhere left to run and no reason to do so. He got to be Dave Jamison, Steelville High School basketball star, again for another night.

DAD FLIPPED on the TV in our motel room. "No Fox News tonight."

I almost shouted out in glee. I couldn't believe it, but instead I gave a chin nod and said, "Cool."

We watched a boxing match instead. Keith Thurman vs. Shawn Porter. Porter was the underdog. We wanted him to win. He didn't. Dad yelled at the TV, "Punch that motherfucker in the mouth."

We stayed up later than we should have. We could have gone to bed after the fight, but we turned the TV off and talked long into the night.

11

The alarm went off at 6:00 a.m., but I was already up. The warmth of the morning sun, which had crept through a divide in the curtains, made an elongated triangle across the bottom half of my bed and had stirred me awake.

Dad sat on the edge of his bed watching Fox News.

Well, that break was short-lived. I wiped sleep from my eyes and walked to the bathroom, rinsed out my mouth, and slipped on basketball shorts and a t-shirt. "Let's go eat."

It would be the last breakfast at the motel. I had grown accustomed to cereal, toast and Nutella, and the bad coffee with a side of grounds that settled at the bottom of the Styrofoam cups. Unlike the two days before, no one was in the buffet line or at any of the tables. Only Dad and me, alone with our thoughts as we picked at our breakfast.

An ornery smile crept across Dad's face. He swallowed down a bite of biscuits and gravy. "Everybody must be sleeping in. Those lazy farts!"

I grinned and started to tell Dad it was early when I

noticed Rhonda behind the counter. I wanted to ask her if she had a cot in the back since she never seemed to leave, but instead I cheers'ed her with my coffee.

Rhonda gave me a wink. "You guys headin' out today? Well, you know where to find me when you need me."

I nodded with a smile before she disappeared somewhere in the back.

Dad raised his eyebrows and grinned. "What'd you think of the reunion?" He looked at me with an expression that said he wanted an honest answer but one that wasn't too harsh.

"It was fun. I enjoyed it."

He raised one eyebrow a little higher.

"Seriously, it was really awesome to meet some of the people you grew up with."

"Boy, I thought that wheelchair was gonna take us out!"

"Yeah, I don't think that guy was prepared for my answer to Lillian's question."

"They're all good people, Joe. They just have a different view on life."

Confirmation that there was a difference between them and me.

"I get it, Dad. Honestly, I really enjoyed them."

And I did. If there was one thing the trip taught me, it was that my judgements aren't always right. I disagreed with most of the folks I'd met along the way, and my notions of them began the moment I heard about their love for Donald Trump. I made assumptions about what they'd think of me if I were my true self, and I cast aspersions about what they thought was right or wrong.

From Rick and Leslie and Silas to the woman from

Wisconsin to the cardboard cutout of James Pershing, I feared our differences. Every time Dad flipped on Fox News, or spoke about Trump turning our country around, I died a little inside.

The truth was, these people were all pieces of me that people like me judged. But really, they were walking complexities. Like Wild Devil Jim and Eliza Morning Star. Like my hillbilliness, my queerness. Dad's hillbilliness and his hidden Blackness. Our political differences.

All of these identities were thrown into a pot, mixed together, and boiled to the surface. And through it all I'd come to realize that our rebel background made us who we are, but our identities had manifested themselves in different ways. Dad's star that had burned out, and mine that always flickered afraid to shine too bright.

People have a right to believe what they want to believe, but we must hold each other accountable and learn to communicate across our differences; to find our bridge to common ground. Only then can we say, "Yeah, I still think you're wrong" or "I respect your perspective, but here's where I differ." We must be willing to try, and we must be prepared to hear the same.

The gifts Dad received from the people from his past have been instilled in me. Our interconnectedness could not be denied. Ta-Nehisi Coates' writing had taught me that the moral arc doesn't bend toward justice like Dr. King preached; it bends toward chaos. Coates said he was more of a Malcolm X than a Martin Luther King, Jr. and that we needed the resistance. I did agree with Coates, in a way; we do need Malcolms. But the trip back to Missouri with Dad taught me that we also need Dr. Kings. I'm more of a

Martin, and those bridges I've discussed—they have to be arcs bending toward justice.

I was lost in my reflections as we ate.

Dad squeezed my knee. "Thanks for coming here with me, Joe."

We gathered up our trash and headed to the room. Between the front desk and the exit sat a display full of glossy tri-folds brochures:

Float Down the Meramec!

Travel Through Historic Steelville!

Explore Meramec Caverns!

Silver Dollar City!

I stopped for a moment and picked up *Historic Steelville*. I brushed my thumb across the letters.

"Want to take it home?" Dad asked.

"Yeah," I said. "I think I will."

WE SHOWERED, packed up, and I stopped to take in one last look at our room before walking away. Home for four days. The motel. The place where Dad and I had disagreements, good laughs, and I became strong enough to accept *us*.

"You ready to leave this place behind?" Dad asked.

I knocked on the wooden desk, for good luck in the future I guess. "Yeah. I'm ready to go back."

In the parking lot of the motel I stood surrounded by a sea of concrete that radiated the blazing sun. My distressed leather, hand-stitched safari travel bag on the ground at my feet, like the day I arrived, unsure of what lay ahead. Then it was easier to poke fun at this place than to take it seriously. I waited for the vagabond in the camo *Jesus Saves* hat to appear, but he never came.

I have this thing where, when I leave places, I imagine I won't ever be back. I soak in the surroundings one more time and allow my body to experience a range of emotions—joy, sadness, longing—and then I'm ready to go. No looking back. It's my way of saying goodbye. Farewell to the experience, and a *see you later* to a time that will never return.

This time, I couldn't *not* look back. As we pulled onto the exit ramp and I-44 directed us back east, I thought about those stretches of road that carried me to my family's past. They brought me there to explore Dad's memory lane, but his past was—and is—my past, too. Those roads took me back to find things I had missed when I thought there was nothing left to explore between us. Those roads will always lead me home to the places time has forgotten. Memories grown over by political bullshit, smothering our similarities, but we pruned it all to bring our life back together again. I traveled those roads with Dad to rediscover not only the past but what will be our present and future. Though I had a deep fear inside of me that going back to our day-to-day lives in Indiana would put us right back to where we were before we came. *Connected* but *strangers*.

Dad and I rode for a long while in silence, lost in our own thoughts. The only sounds were the tires thumping on the Interstate and some twangy country songs that faded into static. We did not talk about Trump one time, even as his campaign signs along the way served as a reminder that he was a part of our lives in Missouri and in Indiana.

We reached our fork in the road in central Illinois,

where I-70 split. One direction led to Chicago and the other way, Indiana.

"Which one do I take?" Dad said frantically.

I chuckled, remembering how I'd done the same thing only a year before when I returned to Indiana after a quick work trip to Illinois. "Follow the signs, Dad. Follow the signs. When you go the wrong way, it takes a long time to get back."

WE PULLED into the drive of my parents' house where Mom greeted us and helped divide our things, taking some toward the house and putting other stuff into the trunk of my car. I stood in the drive and took in the moment. It was a different kind of ritual than my usual saying goodbye. I knew I'd be back there, but I was uncertain if the moment itself would ever return. Life and family; career and political divides; falling into old habits. Would it eventually creep back in to open the gap that's existed between us for twenty-plus years?

I took a deep breath. "Well, I gotta get home."

Dad stood before me with his hands outstretched and on my shoulders. "Are you sure? You can come in and stay awhile." He was not ready for the moment to be over.

"Cory's off and with Sally gone I need to get back to all of that."

Dad nodded and we hugged. "I love you, Joe."

I nodded back and turned toward my car.

Mom and Dad stayed in the drive, waving, until I could no longer see them in my rearview. And it was then that I really cried. I let it all out. The tears fell not out of sadness but out of change. Travel will do that. The path forward from there is never the same. It was my first moment alone in four days, and the first time I felt free to really release my pent-up emotions. I had learned to be brave. Truly brave. I punched my steering wheel right in its mother-fucking mouth and let out a "whew!"

I rolled down the windows and opened the moon roof. I let the evening breeze blow through the car and dry my tears.

BACK HOME, I dropped my bags and embraced Cory. On our entry way table, where I kept my keys and sunglasses, sat a vase with one red rose and a tag that read: *In memory of Sally.*

We sobbed into each other's shoulders and I didn't want to let go. I'd finally escaped an alternate reality and made it back to my safe space. A piece of us had died, and our home would never be the same, but I also felt an urge to be alone and asked Cory if I could.

"Sure thing, sweetie."

I went to our bedroom and began to unpack everything. I grabbed a wad of clothes from my bag and smelled them. The motel. Cigarette smoke from Salem. Fried chicken from the reunion. I threw them toward the hamper. I pulled the *Historic Steelville* brochure from my back pocket and threw it on the dresser.

I flipped on the TV and pulled up the guide. I scrolled until I reached CNN and I hit enter. It had been so many days since I'd seen my precious CNN. I longed for Anderson Cooper, Don Lemon, and the arguments between lesbian liberal Sally Kohn and right-wing Republican pundit Kayleigh McEnany. It would be a much needed detox from all of the Fox News I'd ingested.

But I couldn't do it. It was too much for me. Don't get me wrong, I had not become a Fox News fan, but I realized, as I watched Sally and Kayleigh argue about Donald, Hillary, and Bernie, that it was really . . . stupid. Fox News *and* CNN. Both of them, so smug.

This is not how we win people over and connect.

I clicked off the TV and threw the remote on top of the pile of laundry. I sat on the edge of the bed and fell back to watch the ceiling fan above me turn. I took in a deep breath and exhaled. I closed my eyes and saw scrolling images of four-wheelers and beers and old leather-bound books with family records. I saw disagreements and laughter. Friends from another time. Trump signs. The old church. My dog Sally. Jacob. My old pack of Tiger Cubs. Steve. Life passed me by as a speeding swirl of greens and grays and yellows along an Interstate highway.

And I saw Dad—a memory from when I graduated from college and he put his arm around my neck and pulled me into a headlock hug. He kissed my head and pulled back to look me in the eyes. Tears filled up the edges. I had set, in many ways, destiny back on the path to the straight and wide; fulfilling something he had thought maybe could've happened to him but was never meant to be. He said things would be different for me, but to remember that life could end up being $30,000 a year with a small house, or it could be six figures with people at my every beck and call. Wherever my path led, being brave and taking chances would give me the most out of life. "Just, don't become an asshole."

I opened my eyes and stared up at that same ceiling fan, the one that's hung there for over ten years. As it continued to spin above me, I sat up, reached for my bag, and grabbed my Moleskine. I scribbled: *Hillbilly, Queer*.

12

My phone rang and sent a vibration through my leg. I fought with my pants pocket to retrieve it as I kept one hand on the wheel.

My friend, Kelsey, was on the other end of the line. It had been four months since Missouri with Dad, and this time I was returning to Indiana from a work trip I had taken, alone, to Wisconsin.

Kelsey told me that Gary Younge from *The Guardian* would be in our city for the next month covering the election for a series called *The View from Middletown*, and that he wanted to meet with people on both sides of the political spectrum. But what Gary really hoped to get was two people in the same family who would cancel out each other's vote—and be okay with it. He told me he had spoken to Gary and recommended Dad and me, and he had already given Gary my number and that I should expect a call.

I wanted to do the interview with Gary and I knew I could convince Dad to do it, too, but I was concerned about what he might say or do. I didn't want the world to make fun of him. Whatever we would record with Gary could go out to millions of viewers across the globe, and, depending on the context, I knew people like me would look at Dad and think he was another crazy Trump supporter. This story would not be some post on a Facebook newsfeed that would get lost in the clutter and then disappear. This story would be in newsfeeds of people in every city . . . every state . . . and . . . *shit* . . . every country. *The Guardian* was my turf. Even though Dad had let me onto his turf in Missouri, I was worried about him being on mine.

A month after Dad and I returned from our trip, Hillary and Donald had both received the official nominations from their parties. Dad was still Trump all the way, and I had moved my support over to Hillary, reluctantly. Even though I told Dad when we were in Missouri that I was voting for her, my vote was reserved for Bernie Sanders. But Bernie didn't make it to the end. I wasn't in love with Hillary, but I would not vote for a third party candidate. I saw that as throwing my vote away and paving the path to the White House for Donald Trump. Like so many other of my friends and colleagues, I fell in line and said: *I'm with her.* Even when I really, wasn't.

One observation I'd made since Hillary and Donald had accepted their nominations was the lack of Hillary signs but the abundance of Trump signs. I couldn't help but think most folks were like me, voting for her but not excited enough to go to the trouble to put her sign in the yard. When I'd venture outside of the city limits and into the country, almost every house had a Trump sign.

Trump had said some crazy and racist shit. And the

"locker room talk" between Trump and Billy Bush had been leaked. But with every unbelievable thing he'd say or do, his supporters were still right there behind him. And many of them, including Dad, didn't focus on those things. They focused on jobs and the economy. All of their conversations paralleled the conversations we had in Missouri with Rick, Leslie, and Silas. Their idea of *Make America Great Again* was about the return of jobs with pensions and short commutes.

Since returning from Missouri, I had chosen to spend my Sundays with Dad and Mom. Cory had to work the ER, so I'd do dinner with them. I'd often get frustrated with our conversations when they'd turn to Trump, and I couldn't understand how his rampant sexism and xenophobia was ignored.

Instead of feeling silenced or blowing up, I calmly let Dad know when I disagreed with him and why. He listened but then would tell me he didn't really think Trump was that way. "It's all an act! He only does it for the ratings." Mom, normally apolitical, shook her head and usually sided with me. And when he disagreed with my stance on why Trump was bad for America, I listened.

We did find some common ground. I wanted jobs to come back as much as he did, even though I knew they wouldn't be automotive jobs. I wished we could find our next big thing as automation continued to take over the places where men and women once stood at assembly lines.

Every mile on every road between southern Wisconsin and Indiana, I thought about calling Dad and telling him about this celebrity reporter who wanted to interview us.

But each time I'd begun to dial the number, I started to get a nervous feeling in my throat.

Dad was the tough one, but he'd be vulnerable in my neck of the woods. A deer led to slaughter, and *The Guardian* was the salt lick.

It had become my goal in the months since we had returned from the trip to show people who complained about Trump and his supporters that my own dad was a supporter of him, but he was still my dad and I still loved him. I wanted to express to the world that we must connect across differences with the ones we love because it's the only path to common ground. Our country had become extremely divided during the election cycle. People had started to delete long-standing friends off of Facebook, and post after post in my feed was someone either threatening to move to another country or letting the world know they were no longer speaking to their Trump-supporting brother. We needed to think about converging paths or we would be destined for divergent lives. And that may have been okay for some folks, but for me it wasn't American.

I returned to Indiana late that night. Too late to make a phone call to Dad.

I WOKE THE NEXT MORNING, jumped out of bed, and slid on my glasses. The neon green letters on the digital alarm clock read 9:00 a.m.

"Shit!"

Cory stirred next to me and then went back to sleep.

I knew I had to get a hold of Dad and lock him into the

interview with Gary. Kelsey had told me on our call the day before that Gary's goal was to get the interview recorded over the weekend for a release the following Thursday.

I picked up my cell and dialed Mom and Dad's number. It rang twice and Mom answered.

I told her a reporter from *The Guardian* was in town and that he would like to sit down with Dad and me to talk about the election.

Her hand covered the receiver. "It's J.R. and there's some guy who's interested in talking to the two of you. He's writing an article or a paper or something."

I sighed.

"Your Dad said, 'Okay.' When does this guy want to meet with you?"

I PULLED into Mom and Dad's drive shortly before 2:00 p.m. The garage door was opened, and Dad was inside sweeping the floor. His shirt, with large red and blue letters spelled: *U-S-A*. I looked down at the shirt I had chosen for this occasion: *Drop Stories, Not Bombs*.

Perfect.

We greeted each other with a hug, and as I tried to pull away Dad moved his hand to the back of my head and cupped it—kissing my forehead.

We walked through the doorway into the family room. A room stuck in 1987. The bottom half of the walls were wood paneling and the top half was mauve and gray floral wallpaper. It was the same family room where I watched *Fraggle Rock* and *Saved by the Bell* as a kid. The same room that housed Dad's baptismal Bible. The same room where

Dad called out to me after he found the letter from Steve so many years before, and then sat next to me on the couch as he told me it was okay to be me. A room that had set our path forward for so many things. To my surprise, the TV was not on Fox News. Some old Western played on the screen.

Dad fumbled with the remote. "Here, Joe, we can turn this on to whatever you want."

I chanted over and over in my mind: *Don't turn it to Fox News. Don't turn it to Fox News.*

"You want to watch the news?"

My chest tightened. As much as I had come to find common ground with Dad and find my way back to him by exploring the past, I was not interested in watching *Fox Fucking News* ever again.

"No, that's okay. I want to talk to you about the guy who's coming here in a little bit."

Dad put the remote on the coffee table and took a seat in his easy chair. I sat on the country blue and mauve plaid couch.

"This guy who's coming," I said. "He's from a pretty large paper. He wants to talk to us about the election and how you're voting for Trump and I'm voting for Hillary."

Dad cringed at the sound of her name.

I continued. "He wants us to be very honest. So you can say whatever you want to say, but I want you to know that this paper is fairly liberal. Most of the readers are folks who would never entertain the idea of voting for Trump. So I guess I'm saying I'm not sure what type of questions he might ask you."

Dad looked at me intently and took it all in. He didn't

speak for a moment. I'd begun to think he might back out, and part of me was okay with that. Now that I was there in the flesh with Dad waiting for Gary Younge, I wasn't sure if I actually wanted to go through with the interview. The future can be so uncertain, and here where our turfs met each other was a place where I knew people on both sides would gather and send out rallying cries across the divide.

"But Dad, he really wants to focus in on why you're voting for Trump and why I'm voting for Hillary, and why we would even get along."

"Why we'd get along? Because you're my son. And I'm your dad."

"I know, but some people find that odd."

Dad thought about that for a moment. I could see the confusion in his eyes. There was no confusion in my eyes. I got it. The truth was if you had told me six months before that I'd go on camera with Dad to support his vote for Trump, I would've told you to get out of town. But there we sat, waiting for Gary Younge and his film crew from *The Guardian*.

"So just be yourself. Okay, Dad?"

He agreed.

The doorbell rang.

We opened the door open to Gary Younge and his camera woman, Laurence Mathieu-Léger. As we walked through the kitchen to the family room, Laurence asked if we could move the table so she could get all of her camera equipment through. I was thankful Mom decided to spend the afternoon shopping because she would have been anxious about the house and moving her furniture around.

We settled in the family room. Laurence messed with the vertical blinds and tried to find the right lighting. She instructed us to sit side-by-side on the couch as she set up her camera and did a few test shots. Then she mic'ed us and told us to walk around the house and have casual conversation while she shot some B roll with her other camera.

"You wanna see some of my antlers?" Dad asked Gary as we headed into the garage and Laurence followed us with the camera.

Dad recounted stories of each of the deer he had killed, where, and when. He swapped deer hunting stories, as if he were waiting for us to share stories back in return. Gary and I stood next to each other in silence as Dad continued on from one rack to the next. Dad didn't seem concerned that a liberal outlet was there to interview him, or what they might do with that interview. Instead, he lit up from excitement for getting to have the spotlight again for a moment.

Then Gary asked the question I knew would eventually come: "Dave, tell me why you want to vote for Donald Trump."

I took a deep breath. Nervous. This was it, Dad was in *my* version of Steelville.

Dad looked at me, then he looked at the camera. He turned back toward the shelf with his deer antlers. "Trump. I always thought he was an arrogant SOB. But then, some of my friends around the deer camp said, 'You better vote for Trump. Get the jobs back to America.' So I started giving him another look and liked what I saw."

He paused and waited for Gary to respond. Gary didn't and motioned with a nod for Dad to continue.

"Let's go back in the house and we can continue the conversation in there," Dad said.

Back in the family room, Laurence readjusted our mics as Dad continued with his stories. "Hey, Gary. Did Joe tell you I'm part Black?"

I cringed. Gary Younge is Black.

Gary laughed, and with a puzzled look on his face he asked Dad to tell him more.

"I'm a sixteenth Black, one-eighth Cherokee Indian, and the rest is German and Scotch-Irish."

Well, it was obvious Dad had embraced the confirmation of his newfound identity. I remembered this was *The Guardian* and hoped viewers wouldn't consider us to be in the same category as Rachel Doležal, the woman who was born white but presented herself to the world as if she were Black. I was certain they'd cut that part, though. There was no real reason to keep it.

Gary raised an eyebrow but continued to smile curiously.

Laurence instructed us to take our places back on the couch. Dad in the middle, Gary and me on either side. "Okay, ready, action," she said.

Gary started. "Dave, tell me, again, who you plan to vote for next month."

"I think I'm gonna vote for Trump. Get America back. Middle class jobs and everything. I think that's what people are looking for. Jobs."

"Do you think those jobs are really coming back?"

Dad paused and turned his head to the side in thought. "Nope, I don't. I don't think there's much hope in getting those good paying factory jobs back . . . I think they're gone."

Dad looked down at the floor. I saw a sadness in his eyes. The same sadness I had seen when we drove to Missouri and he told me about his high school athletic records being boxed up, and how his life had changed when he got kicked out of Bible college. They were eyes that had seen the what-might-have-beens but never took the opportunity.

I reached over and squeezed his knee as he had done for me so many times before to validate my feelings. Then, with a deep breath, I said, "You know, folks who did not have a college degree were brought up from the south to work jobs that were more blue-collar. They see Trump almost as their savior because, even though he goes completely off script and talks about women and all of that, others see hope in his message. And Obama had hope in his message and that's where I see the similarity—between what we saw happening in this country in '08 and what we see now."

Dad grabbed my knee and gave it a return squeeze. We looked into each other's eyes, and I almost started to cry but I didn't. And it would have been okay if I had. I didn't need to punch life in the mouth. We don't need to fight the ones we love. We need empathy.

Dad looked at me with pride. Not equal parts shock and pride. Only pride. And I was proud of him for doing this and standing his ground. I guess, I was proud of us for being brave together. I survived his turf, and he had now survived mine.

Laurence stopped filming and we each reached under our shirts and undid our mics.

"That was really great, guys. I think I have enough footage to piece something together for our Thursday release," she said.

Dad and I helped Laurence with her equipment and then we walked her and Gary to the front door. We said our goodbyes and I stared out the glass storm door until their SUV was no longer in sight.

Dad and I grabbed either end of the kitchen table and maneuvered it back and forth until we felt comfortable with where we thought it had been.

I leaned against the kitchen table. "Thank you for doing the interview."

After all of our nights together in Missouri watching the news, *we* were now the news. Our lives were a production, but not staged.

Kelsey texted me on Thursday morning: DID YOU SEE THE ARTICLE AND THE VIDEO? YOU'RE FAMOUS!

I hadn't. In all honesty, the time from Saturday to Thursday had flown by so fast I'd almost forgotten we'd done the interview with Gary.

I flipped open my laptop and went to *The Guardian's* homepage. Front and center was a large photo of Dad, Gary, and me on the couch with the caption: TRUMP SPEAKS TO US IN A WAY OTHER PEOPLE DON'T.

Shit. My goddamned picture is right above this caption. People are going to think I'm a Trump supporter!

I clicked on the link that led to an article about all of the Trump supporters Gary had encountered in our community, including Dad. The video of our interview was embedded front and center at the top. The screenshot was the image of us on the couch, made even bigger than it was on *The Guardian's* homepage.

The interview was released in two segments. First, the article, and the second as a standalone video titled: FATHER BACKS TRUMP, SON BACKS CLINTON: WE AGREE TO DISAGREE.

The first caption for the article, about Trump speaking to us in a way that other people don't, got more traction.

I clicked on the video and it opened with B-roll footage of Mom and Dad's street, the golden fall sun glistened through leaves that had not yet fallen from the trees. Somber music played in the background.

Gary's voice spoke over the music. "Like the rest of the country, there's a generational divide in Muncie. Here most of the younger people I've met are supporting Hillary while their parents are supporting Trump. That's the case with J.R., a scholar and motivational speaker, and his dad, Dave, who's retired."

More B-roll continued but this time of Mom and Dad's family room, and then I heard, "I'm a sixteenth Black, one-eighth Cherokee Indian, and the rest is German and Scotch-Irish."

Well, shit, they kept it.

I continued to watch and, while some key points were cut, what was pieced together was a fairly good representation of Dad and me. *Connected* but not *strangers.*

Within a day, the article and the video had been shared on social media thousands of times and got nearly a thousand comments on *The Guardian's* site. Of course, I did exactly what everyone tells you not to do: I read them.

That section of any online outlet is the seventh level of

hell. People with avatars and aliases decided this was their space to voice the most vile and outrageous statements possible. They fought with each other, they made blanket statements about the article, and every now and then their arguments were broken up by a bot advertising half-price handbags.

Most of the comments under the article were against Trump supporters in general, and then I came across one comment that was directed at Dad and me.

GOOD INTERVIEW. GOOD PEOPLE.

But another replied: ONE OUT OF TWO ISN'T BAD.

Snarky. *Were they talking about Dad or me?*

Several more posters considered Dad to be stupid, ignorant, and not knowing what he talked about. Even though *The Guardian* is a fairly liberal outlet, a few took jabs at me.

One wrote: THE SON IN THIS PIECE IS VERY CONDESCENDING. WHAT A DEPRESSING VIDEO.

I eventually landed on this post: I WISH MORE PEOPLE IN THE WORLD HAD THE ATTITUDE OF THE FATHER AND SON IN THE FILM CLIP.

I decided I wanted to be left with that positive note, and I climbed out of the seventh level of hell. I had survived Dad's turf, but could I survive my own?

I called Mom and Dad's house and Mom answered. She told me they had seen the piece from *The Guardian* and that Dad thought it was "neat." I asked her to make sure that Dad didn't read the comments under the article.

"Comments?"

I told her never mind and hung up knowing that she immediately went to the comments section. But if she and Dad did sit for hours reading each of them, they never said anything else about it or the article.

I guess Dad had survived my turf after all.

13

THE NIGHT of the election I gathered with Kelsey and Gary Younge at the Downtown Farm Stand in Muncie, an all organic grocery store and deli owned by my friend, Dave.

In the two weeks since our interview together with Gary, Dad had hinted at the possibility of switching his vote. He told me that some of Trump's comments about women and minorities were starting to get to him, and that if Trump kept it up he might have no other choice but to vote for Hillary.

Farm Stand Dave rolled a flat screen TV strapped to a cart out into an open area of the deli. Kelsey and I sat at one table, Gary at another by himself, and Dave stood—every so often pacing from the deli to the Fair Trade coffee aisle back to the deli. His eyes never once left the TV.

We all sipped our organic, GMO-free beer and watched the returns.

The night started out hopeful. Before the coverage began we laughed, toasted, and talked about how historic the night would be. The first woman President of the United States would be elected, and we were there to watch history.

But early on in the coverage, it became clear that something was not right. State after state went to Trump.

Wolf Blitzer announced, "It's too early to call, but our estimates indicate that Donald J. Trump has won . . ."

Then, like a broken record—insert state. And before long, as much as we didn't want to admit it, it seemed evident that Trump would be our next president.

"You don't think he'll actually win, right?" I said to the group.

Gary looked over at me. "I think he's won. I've seen this before. This is Brexit all over again." He shook his head.

I knew he was right. Since Missouri with Dad, I'd had on my mind that Trump might actually win. My liberal friends disagreed. Many of them said there was no way he would win, and they never even entertained the idea. One day, when I speculated what life after the election might look like with Trump as our president, one of my friends valley-girl-laughed: "No way! I'm not even going to give him a thought."

But rural working class folks, like Dad, had grown in their momentum and had clearly spoken. I hated that it had come to this. Our divides had boiled over and led to this moment; more proof of how far apart we are from one another. It was proof of a divide most didn't know was so vast. But I saw this divide building momentum. I felt it coming on over the past twenty years, and watched it arrive as I traveled back with Dad, explored his turf, and returned to my own. We may have come together as Dad and son, but to everyone else like us we were still worlds apart.

Farm Stand Dave did one last pace from the Fair Trade coffee aisle to the TV, and then he clicked it off. The screen went black. "Yeah, I'm not going to watch the end. Sorry, guys, I'm headed home to be with my family."

We gathered up our glasses and put them into Dave's bussing station. Gary and I slapped hands, slid our palms in opposite directions toward each other's fingers, ending with a snap before we let go. I thanked him for sitting down with Dad and me. I wouldn't see Gary again. He left Muncie the next morning to head back to England.

One by one, we walked out of the Farm Stand and headed in different directions.

THE NEXT MORNING I awoke to breaking news that Donald Trump would become the 45th President of the United States. On loop, all of the news station played his acceptance speech:

I've just received a call from Secretary Clinton. She congratulated us — it's about us — on our victory, and I congratulated her and her family on a very, very hard-fought campaign. I mean, she fought very hard. Hillary has worked very long and very hard over a long period of time, and we owe her a major debt of gratitude for her service to our country. I mean that very sincerely. Now it's time for America to bind the wounds of division; we have to get together. To all Republicans and Democrats and Independents across this nation, I say it is time for us to come together as one united people. It's time. I pledge to every citizen of our land that I will be president for all Americans, and this is so important to me.

I wasn't sure I totally believed him, but he was now our president-elect and at least he made an effort to recognize the country was divided. I mean, a division he helped create, or at least brought to the surface. Our nation's chasm was revealed and Trump was the monster that called out of the crack. *That* he would not admit. But as much as I wasn't excited to know he'd be our next leader, I had some hope in his message. We *were* a nation divided. But if I could see the similarities between people like Rick and Leslie and Silas and Dad and me, and others could try to do the same, maybe we could move past this horrible election cycle and come together as a country after all.

On my drive to the office, I dialed Mom and Dad's number a few times and never hit the call button. I had thought of Dad the entire day on Election Day. I wanted to call him so badly, but I never mustered the courage to do it. I had lost my bravery, I guess. Partly, even though I assumed he had, I didn't want to hear him actually say he had voted for Trump. I defended his right to vote for that man, but still it felt personal. Like my life as a gay man wasn't enough to keep Dad from running back toward something that had long been gone. A nostalgia for something that doesn't exist. One that had nice window dressings, but underneath all of it was a truth that shone so brightly people were blinded by it. They hadn't seen the xenophobia, homophobia, and every other phobia that projected outward. They only saw what they wanted to see on the surface. And maybe I shouldn't have been so open to giving *that* a free pass.

Maybe coming together will be harder than I thought.

When I arrived to the office, my colleagues were all gathered in the conference room. A box of Kleenex sat in the middle of the long wooden table. They were all in tears and already deep into a conversation about the results of the election. I stood in the doorway and listened to their exchange.

"I can't believe it. I just can't. This can't be real."

"I talked to my boyfriend last night about building a bomb shelter. We've already started pricing it out."

"I wonder if Canada will consider us refugees."

Concern after concern, they expressed what the new normal might be like. A post-apocalyptic fascist world.

One colleague wiped her eyes and cleared her throat. "I've heard the campus is suggesting we put signs in our windows letting students know this is a safe space to come talk about their fears and to, you know, have a place to be angry and cry. I think we should do it."

"Absolutely not," I retorted.

They all looked on in shock and horror. One colleague's Kleenex suspended in midair between her cheek and her eye.

I cleared my throat but didn't make eye contact. "Look, I'm as upset as the next person about the results of this election, but what does that say to students who *did* vote for Trump if we're showing favoritism to the students who are unhappy with the outcome?"

I again thought, as I had so often over the last few months: *Who have I become?*

My mind drifted to Rick, Leslie, and Silas—and to Dad. They'd all been on my mind the past few days.

Since the interview with Gary, I had been labeled as a

Trump sympathizer by some, and others said I had given his supporters a free pass. And I knew this wasn't helping my case. But I also knew if we put a sign in our window and let the world know our office was a safe space for those who were unhappy with the results of the election, we'd never start closing the gap that existed. A gap I knew couldn't totally be closed, but even when cracks still existed it didn't mean we had to be assholes to each other.

I was as worried as they were. I worried about my safety as a gay man in a world where Mike Pence was now our vice president. A world where Jacobs can throw canisters at the heads of gay boys, and men in rumbling trucks can yell "faggot" out their windows. Trump had given rise to people who felt emboldened to hate. But that's not Dad or Silas or Rick or Leslie. People needed their safe spaces, but so did Dad. Who would protect people like him from people like me?

My colleagues didn't talk to me for the rest of the day.

ON MY DRIVE HOME, I pulled out my phone and dialed the number for Mom and Dad. It rang once, twice—

Dad answered.

"I'm assuming we cancelled out each other's vote after all," I said. "Maybe that was meant to be."

He laughed. "Maybe it was."

We sat in silence. It was probably only a few seconds, but it felt like an eternity. A proverbial knee squeeze between us. Miles separated us, and cell towers pinging from one to the next could have disconnected us at any moment, but in the quiet, with Dad, I felt more *connected* and understood than ever before. No longer *strangers*.

I wasn't searching for what to say next. I wasn't trying to build up bravery for anything. I wasn't flexing my muscles to show my machismo. I wasn't silenced though we sat in silence. I'd already found my voice by exploring our past. No urge to punch any mother-fuckers in the mouth anymore.

Vivid images passed through my mind of all that came before and all that would come after. I thought about walking away from my home in 1997 for college, and everything that had changed in the twenty years that spanned the past and the present with Dad. All of the ups and downs and growing apart to find each other again.

I thought about coming out. Steve. My marriage to Cory. My liberal friends with whom I've felt at home with for so long. My own safe spaces. My turf.

I thought about my hate for Donald Trump and Fox News and everyone who stood for those institutions. I thought about Jacob and that evening in his truck. I guess you could say, my unsafe spaces.

I thought about when Dad told me how he had said goodbye to his Dad, in a jail cell on a cold March night in a year where winter had lasted longer than it should have. On that last night of his life, Grandpa Harrison lay shivering alone. He hadn't had a drink in days after being picked up for a minor infraction. Dad came to tell him that he had to give it up. He asked him why he kept doing this to himself and their family, and Grandpa Harrison told him he loved the drink more than he loved his life. The drink is what made him feel alive. Dad left that jail not knowing he would never see his Dad again. They never got the chance to connect; to find their common ground.

I heard Old Lady Baker's voice remind me that there is beauty and peace all around even when the world may be going to shit. And the catharsis of that was enough to not give up.

I saw the rock I threw into the baptismal creek of crystal blue water at Mount Olive, and with each ripple I counted I allowed myself to forgive every one of those kids from church and school, and Dad too, for all the things he said about the gays at a time when he didn't know his son was one of them. And as each ripple hit the edge of the Earth and began to break apart, I counted all of the times Dad was brave enough to accept me despite our differences. *Could I be brave enough to accept my Trump-voting dad?*

. . . I was.

In those flashes of life past and life future, I saw Wild Devil Jim and Eliza Morning Star. Though I never knew them in life, I will forever feel them beating in my heart. They gave us our rebel genes. The courage to not be boxed in. Dad and I shared the same complex history, but our lived experiences had made our paths different. And that's okay. Even when we found each other on opposite sides of the aisle, we'd become strong enough to reach out and touch each other through the divide that lay between us. A conservative, a liberal. A Baptist, an atheist. A hillbilly, a queer.

My mind skipped ahead to twenty years down the road: 2036. Dad, ninety-two. Me, fifty-seven. So many miles to cover between now and then. I hoped I could keep us on the right path, even if the flow of traffic in our lanes moved at different paces.

What will it be like? Who will be president? Will Dad still be alive?

I thought about all of the people I would come to know, and all of the people I could lose. I thought about if I ever had my own son, what he would be like in twenty years. Would he be like me, or different? Would he know his roots? Would he pick up this book and ask questions, or would he look at his old Dad and have suspicions because of all the ways we were different?

I hoped he would do what I did for my dad and what my dad did for me.

Listen. Forgive. Learn.

And, through those lessons, I hoped he might teach the world to do the same.

I took a deep breath and said the only thing that made sense in that moment: "I love you, Dad."

EPILOGUE

IT HAS BEEN over four years since I took the trip to Missouri with my dad, and what a strange trip it has been from then to now. In that time our country has become more divided; racism, homophobia, and transphobia are rampant; and as I write this note we are in the middle of a global pandemic where leaders haven't used science as a trusted source to guide us out. Some days it feels like 2020 has been a final chapter in the United States of America.

I could make this about Trump or Biden; Republican versus Democrat; or the 2020 election cycle. But I won't other than to say, because I think some folks will be curious, my dad did not vote for Trump in 2020. He did support his presidency almost until the end, but ultimately it took the mishandling of the pandemic, and the death of hundreds of thousands of Americans, for Dad to decide that Trump did not have the best interest in mind for the future of our country. This woke Dad up to other realities as well, and in his own words: "That Trump is full of himself and full of shit."

But if Dad had voted for Trump, would I still talk to him? Absolutely. And that's all I'll say about Trump because this isn't about him. This is about us; the people.

The 2016 trip to Dad's hometown was an opportunity to traverse the roads of his life to learn what made him who he was; to see his ups and downs; and to discover that the ones closest to us—despite the pain either has caused—are the best jumping off points for empathy.

I feel fortunate to have Dad in my life; someone so different from me, but someone who shares my history. The thing I recognized most as I wrote *Hillbilly Queer* is how similar our lives actually are. How we've both encountered many challenges, but even more moments of perseverance. On the surface, we may seem like complete opposites—I've never seen Dad wear three-inch inseam chinos, and he's never seen me put in a dip of tobacco—but both of us have had hurtful words thrown our way, we've had chances to be the star, and we took the opportunity to tread on one another's turfs and survived to tell the tale.

Writing *Hillbilly Queer* was not only an exploration of bravery, but a journey to decide what is important to keep in our lives and what is important to let go. What is negotiable, and what is not. It was a discovery of identity and what makes us who we are. When I dug down deep to find the tragedies that have festered under the surface of our lives, it was an opportunity to realize that the shame I felt over my hillbilly roots was similar to the shame I felt as that boy in the locker room who realized he was indeed different from everyone else. Similar to the shame Dad carried with him from his own childhood in Steelville to his adulthood in Indiana. It was cathartic to write about, and it was an opportunity to move on. I hope our story is one that can help you do the same.

Like wise Old Lady Baker said, in the end our stories and lived experiences are what we have, and they are the things that will unite us in the gray. Over the past few years, what Dad and I have found on our journey is that we must continue to hold each other accountable and learn to communicate across our differences because our country depends on it. Only when we can sit across from one another can we change the path forward. It's not up to the president or anyone in Congress, it's up to us.

To some people, Dad and I are a hillbilly and a queer. To others, we're just Dave and J.R. I guess it depends on how you choose to view the world.

DISCUSSION GUIDE

J.R. Jamison has spoken at conferences, libraries, universities, and speakers' series around the nation and the world, both in-person and virtually. Would you like J.R. to meet with your group? Learn more at jrjamison.com/speaking.

If you're teaching *Hillbilly Queer*, or discussing it with members of your book club, consider using the following questions, prompts, and activities as a guide.

Questions:

1. Which character in *Hillbilly Queer* do you most relate to and why?

2. Talk about the first time you heard the word *hillbilly*.

3. Talk about the first time you heard the word *queer*.

4. Social class is a major theme in *Hillbilly Queer*, and it is threaded throughout flashback and present-day scenes. Connected to this theme, J.R. writes about education being the great equalizer but also the great divider.

- How do you perceive the relationship between education and social class?

5. LGBTQ+ acceptance has evolved over the past two decades, and as J.R.'s story unfolds we see this through his relationship with his dad, Dave.

- Are there parts of your identity that others have come to accept over time?

6. Race is a social construct but racism is not.

- What role did race and racism play in this story?
- How did race and racism impact the identities of the characters and what were the implications?
- Is racism uniquely American?—or it a global issue?

7. The intersections of identity play a critical role in the narrative arc of *Hillbilly Queer*.

- What advantages do the characters have due to identity?
- What disadvantages do they have?

- Do J.R. and Dave come to accept the parts of themselves they have hidden?

8. J.R. writes about understanding privilege as being a privilege itself—reserved for those with the means and access to materials/knowledge.

- Do you think this is a fair assessment?

9. As the story of *Hillbilly Queer* unfolds—

- What similarities did you see between J.R.'s and Dave's stories?
- What differences did you see?
- Did the characters develop and evolve over time?

10. Think back to the 2016 election cycle.

- Who is someone you disagreed with politically but still loved?
- Would you have taken a trip with them at the height of the 2016 election?
- What about taking a similar trip at the height of the 2020 election?

Freewriting Prompts:

Freewriting is a tool for reflection. Topics are given, and the writer writes whatever comes to mind during a period of time without stopping (even if it's only "I don't know what to say . . ." over and over until something about the topic surfaces). The goal here is to write freely without an editor's mind. Using the following 10 topics, choose five and write for five minutes on each. Then, with a partner or in a small group, discuss patterns and similarities that emerged from your free writes.

1. Political versus cultural differences.
2. Religion.
3. Bullying.
4. Sexuality.
5. Racism in America.
6. Classism in America.
7. Privilege.
8. Resistance.
9. The great divide.
10. Connecting across difference.

Write Your Own Story:

Tiptoeing into someone else's world takes courage and empathy. Using The Facing Project's model of writing/storytelling as a guide (see: http://facingproject.com/story-submission/) sit down with someone else who has a vastly different view than you, have a conversation, and write a 750-1,000 word story from their point of view (and they can do the same with you). Then do the following:

1. Use the story as an opportunity for further discussion.
2. Submit the story to The Facing Project for

others to learn from your experience/story (using the link above).

3. Post excerpts from your story on social media using the hashtags: #hillbillyqueerchallenge #facingproject #mystory.

ACKNOWLEDGMENTS

When I was a kid, I stared out across the fields of corn in Cowan, Indiana, and daydreamed that one day I would sit down to write the great American novel. I imagined typing out each word and phrase at my oak Sauder desk with the keyboard pullout, where a book would appear before my eyes in a matter of hours. It seemed so simple. Truthfully, writing a book was one of the hardest things I've ever done, and it took me until I was nearly 40 years old to do it. It was a four-year journey filled with coffee, and even more coffee, and sometimes tears. There was laughter, too, and memories made that I will never forget. Luckily for me, writing a book was also not a solo task. Every book you've ever picked up and loved had an entire team of people behind it. This book was no different.

First and foremost, I want to thank my husband, Cory Pippin, who allowed me the time and space to write, and for handling my many breakdowns with grace, love, and kindness. We made it!

My literary agent, Julie Stevenson at Massie & McQuilkin in New York City, who believed in this book from the start and helped shape the final draft. I really hit the lottery when she found me in the slush. Julie has been my champion, and friend, since the first day she picked up *Hillbilly Queer*.

The entire team at The Facing Project Press who fight daily for stories like mine to be told: Lori Kniffin, Jay Moorman, Anna Kathryn Barnes, Stephanie Fisher, Sue Godfrey, Lauren Instenes, Shantanu Suman, Alex Sventeckis, and Garima Verma. Also, an extra special shout out to Shantanu and Emma Fulkerson for designing the gorgeous cover that I've loved from the moment I saw it, and to Garima for being a public relations BOSS.

Kelsey Timmerman, my editor and brother from another mother, who told me I had a book when I thought I had only enough for an essay. Kelsey pushed me to try harder, even when I kicked and screamed. Thank you for holding down the fort at The Facing Project while I wrote and edited, and for being my partner-in-crime when it comes to storytelling on the page, stage, and over the airwaves. However, this is a gentle reminder that you still owe me 452 coffees.

All of my beta and sensitivity readers, but especially: Gail Werner, who provided invaluable feedback on reconstructing dialogue for memoir; Christopher Schelling whose early advice ultimately reshaped some parts of *Hillbilly Queer*; and Monica Engle Thomas who copyedited and made sure I watched my tenses. (Also, thank you, Monica, for telling me the book made you laugh and ugly cry even when you didn't have to give that feedback, but it came when I needed it most and kept me going.) Likewise, I'd be remiss if I didn't mention Jane Friedman, who is the industry leader on the "business (side) of writing"—I've enjoyed learning from you and appreciated the time you spent with me to provide advice.

Marie Massie & Rob McQuilkin: It is an honor to be one of the writers represented by your agency.

Outside of the team who helped with this book, teachers never get enough credit for molding lives. I would have never made it through the halls of Cowan without Ms. Janice Garner, who took me into her Chemistry classroom and gave me a TA position to keep me out of Study Hall and away from the hands of bullies. I didn't know squat about Chemistry, but I was the best paper-grader ever (spoiler: I used a key she created, so really I only *checked* or *x'ed* answers). Also, all of my theatre teachers who gave me a safe space on the stage and encouraged me to find my voice: Mrs. Linda Weaver, Mrs. Elaine Barr, and Mr. Rodney Overla. A special shout out to fellow Cowan student and queer, Holly Hudson, who vowed to break the necks of all my bullies. She never had to, but the sentiment helped me survive. And to Jason Love, who was one of my biggest bullies but reached out twenty-three years later to apologize; though I had forgiven him long ago that apology meant the world to me, and I'm happy to have a newfound friend and ally.

The entire crew at The Caffeinery made sure my single origin black eye, with a little ice in the bottom, waited for me each morning as I wrote and edited *Hillbilly Queer*. I could not have made it through this process without you. Special thanks to the owners, Frank and Lauren Reber.

The entire team at Indiana Public Radio has brought my voice and stories from The Facing Project to listeners across the globe via NPR One and PRX: Sean Ashcraft (my producer), Dan Lutz, Michelle Kinsey, Lori Georgi, Andrea Lutz, Angie Rapp, and Stephanie Wiechmann, among others—you all are the best!

Friends from the Midwest Writers Workshop—Hallie Rufener (who will someday be known to the world as writer Kate Henry), Eric Percak, Stephen Mortland, Ashley C. Ford, Shelly Gage, Rena Olsen, Marjorie Brimer, Jama Bigger, Irene Fridsma, Terri Devries, Garrett Hutson—thank you all for your support.

Barbara Bogue, who took 19-year-old me under her wing and taught me how to hone my craft. I learned so much from you, and your spirit can be found in my writing and community-based work.

Sammy, my lucky Lhasa Apso, was the best dog ever, and he sat between my legs for the entire journey of this book (literally!) and went on runs with me when I needed a mental break. He also died in my arms of lung cancer not long after I finished the final edits. I will always love you, Sammy-Sam. Thank you for teaching me patience. I continue to use this gift with your new brother, J.J.

Matt and Christina Capps spent a long weekend with Cory and me in St. Pete, Florida, when I was deep in edits but desperately needed to get away. Justin and Chy Renick and Kristi Fierce took care of Sammy while we were gone. Thank you, all!

Lindsey Adkins always knew when I needed a porch night.

My siblings, both real and chosen, have helped shape who I am as a person and, ultimately, as a storyteller: James, Julie, Stacia, Debbie, Justin, Stacey, Jason, Tim, Tyler,

Tonia, Ross, Chase, Brock, Erin, and Kelsey. Y'all know me better than anyone (for better or for worse).

My in-laws, Gary and Jama Pippin, who created one of the biggest joys in my life.

Last but certainly not least, my mom, Bernie Jamison, and my dad—Dave. This book would not exist without you. Thank you for my hillbilly roots and for letting me blossom as a queer.

ABOUT THE AUTHOR

J.R. JAMISON is a founder of
The Facing Project, a national
organization that creates a more
understanding and empathetic
world through stories that
inspire action. He also co-hosts
The Facing Project Radio Show
on NPR. His work has been
featured in *The Guardian,*
Harlem World Magazine, The
Huffington Post, and in
numerous literary journals. He
lives in Muncie, Indiana, with his husband Cory and their
dog, J.J.

Photo by Matt Howell

To learn more about J.R. and his writing, follow him
online at jrjamison.com and on Twitter & Instagram,
@jr_jamison.

ABOUT THE FACING PROJECT PRESS

The Facing Project Press is an imprint of The Facing Project, a 501(c)(3) nonprofit that creates a more understanding and empathetic world through storytelling. The organization provides tools and a platform for everyday individuals to share their stories, connect across differences, and begin conversations using their own narratives as a guide. The Facing Project has engaged more than 7,500 volunteer storytellers, writers, and actors who have told more than 1,500 stories that have been used in grassroots movements, in schools, and in government to inform and inspire action. Stories from The Facing Project are published in books through The Facing Project Press and are regularly performed on *The Facing Project Radio Show* on NPR.

Beginning with the publishing of *Hillbilly Queer*, The Facing Project Press will acquire memoirs and narrative nonfiction that strive to live out the mission of The Facing Project through *The Empathy Prize*. Learn more at facingproject.com.

facebook.com/thefacingproject

twitter.com/facingproject

instagram.com/facingproject